RANDOM TABLES
CITIES AND TOWNS

The Game Master's Companion for Developing
Inns, Shops, Taverns, Settlements, and More

Dr. Timm Woods

Published in the United States by:
ULYSSES PRESS
P.O. Box 3440
Berkeley, CA 94703
www.ulyssespress.com

ISBN: 978-1-64604-009-4
Library of Congress Control Number: 2019951343

Printed in the United States by Kingery Printing Company
10 9 8 7 6 5 4 3 2

Acquisitions editor: Casie Vogel
Managing editor: Claire Chun
Editor: Miriam Jones
Proofreader: Renee Rutledge
Cover and interior design/layout: what!design @ whatweb.com
Artwork from shutterstock.com: dice (cover/interior) © kericanfly; town (cover) © Firstear; page border © 100ker; © Artur Balytskyi, pages 10, 31, 41, 57, 61, 69, 73, 91, 116, 125, 155; © Pavila pages 15, 107, 114, 122; © Zdenek Sasek, pages 21, 47, 51; © Vorobiov Oleksii 8, pages 22, 32, 39, 29; © KateChe, page 24; © Medvedka, page 43; © Roman Bykhalov, page 45; © Varlamova Lydmila, page 46; © ArtMari, pages 70, 104, 129, 133, 139, 144, 163; © truhelen, page 85; © Golden Shrimp, page 96; © HQ Vectors Premium Studio, page 132; © Rawpixel.com, page 135; © AVA Bitter, page 141; © mamita2, page 156; © NAtaLima, page 164; © Rustic, page 166

To my family, my original adventuring party

Contents

People. 58

Property 126

Acknowledgments 167

About the Author 167

Introduction

Hello and welcome, traveler!

It looks like you could use some rest! Gaze around this beautiful tavern; take in the sights, the sounds, the music, the ambiance ...

... actually, it's pretty boring. There's ... a guy. And ... a candle. And ... some drinks?

What's this? You're a Game Master, you say? A storyteller? And you're actually running a role-playing game right now? This is *your* imaginary tavern? And you have a table full of players who want to know what happens next? Oh no—they're about to enter the tavern, and you weren't expecting them to do that! It's not ready!

Never fear. Take a deep breath, because you hold in your hands the key to unlimited city-based adventures.

Every Game Master gets stumped on occasion by some unexpected course of action that the player-characters have taken. Improvising whole scenes on the spot can be tough, but with the help of this book, it just got a lot easier. Using these tables, a storyteller can generate on-the-fly details to make any tavern, shop, or street feel alive and vibrant. Towns and cities are especially prone to player-driven storytelling; now you can feel prepared for when a character decides to carouse through town, see the sights, or otherwise go rogue!

How to Use This Book

Whether you need that initial spark of inspiration or already have the beginning of an idea that you want to flesh out, this book has something to offer you when designing your own fantasy town.

Let's say, for example, that your players have put you on the spot. They're paying a surprise visit to that tavern you told them about, The Burning Barrow. Unfortunately, you didn't expect them to reach the Barrow until next week's session! As the storyteller, you know what important plot events are supposed to happen there; but the details and the atmosphere are all completely flat, and you've got less than a minute to cook them up!

But a minute is all that you'll need. First, flip to page 74, pick up the d20, and roll to generate some Tavern Patrons to fill up that common room. Turn to pages 158 and 162, and roll to find out what food and drink options are available here. You can even generate a random stuffed head or two to mount over the bar by flipping to page 166 and rolling there. Then, add in a unique bard's song (page 82) and give the singer a quirk or two (page 86). Use as many or as few of the tables as you want! Before you know it, you'll have a tavern that will catch your players' attention, paint a vivid and descriptive image, and probably encourage more than a few side-quests and shenanigans.

When you feel stumped, at a creative block, or just out of ideas in general, this book can help launch you back into creativity and fun. Just find the question that you're looking to answer, like:

What's in that nobleman's pocket that the thief just picked? Who lives across the street from the local blacksmith? How is the bartender feeling today, and what's on the menu?

Once you have your question, flip to the relevant table and grab your dice. Each table will tell you what to roll, whether it's a d20 (a 20-sided die), a d100 (a 100-sided die), or some other dice. Some tables might ask you to add numbers to your roll. Just follow the instructions, roll the dice, and refer to the tables in this book to see what exciting, surprising results you've generated.

All ideas within these tables are suggestions! Use them as inspiration for your own stories, or build entire adventures using random rolls, or save the book for when you need to really surprise the players (and yourself)! There's no wrong way to play; and whatever you don't like, just re-roll! In just a few seconds, you'll have dozens of vivid scenes and encounters waiting to play out!

Places

Town Sizes (d6)

Not all towns are equal, and there is a world of difference between a sleepy cluster of houses and a bustling seaport. If you're generating a random town or settlement, this is where to start. Roll here to find out what size of town the characters will find.

Size	Description
1: Metropolis	This is a major capital or trading port, a center of economic control and political authority. The citizens here set the standard for technology, culture, and lifestyle in the surrounding region, and the influence of this city can be seen on the global scale; goods and services of every kind may be found here. Crowds are everywhere and inescapable, and individuals are quickly and easily lost in a sea of hundreds of thousands of faces.
2: Large City	This large population center exercises a major influence over the surrounding region, likely laying claim to the land as its own. Many of the harder-to-find commodities are available here, as well as the vices of the big city. This place is known throughout the world and likely has a reputation that precedes it.
3: Small City	The bustling of crowds can occasionally be seen in a city like this. Many of the amenities and luxuries of civilization are available here, and the city is well-protected by some kind of army and/or government. Thousands or even tens of thousands of souls call this place home.
4: Town	This is a proper established settlement, likely with walls and/or other fortifications to guard the general population, which may number in the thousands. The town has a thriving economy with many industries, and while people recognize most faces, they likely don't know everyone's name.
5: Village	This small settlement has a very rustic quality, and the people here are often outnumbered by the wild animals and livestock. But the village manages to support a variety of different shops and industries, thanks to the farmers and other people who flock in from the countryside on a weekly basis.
6: Hamlet	This quaint little community might not have more than one hundred souls that call it home, and no more than a few dozen standing structures. Nonetheless, the folks who live here are fiercely loyal, having close ties to the land and to each other, and are likely part of the first generation to settle in the region.

Town Governments (d20)

A town's governmental structure can have a major impact on characters who seek to interfere with the region's political machinations, or who simply get on the wrong side of the law or the ruling authorities. Roll here to see what kind of government the town has in place.

1: Civilian Autocracy

2: Magocracy

3: Noble Oligarchy

4: Merchant Oligarchy

5: Tyranny

6: Republic

7: Democracy

8: Shadow Council

9: Crime Syndicate

10: Theocracy

11: Feudal Monarchy

12: Parliamentary Monarch

13: Collective

14: Provincial Imperial Rule

15: Public Council/Town Meeting

16: Military Dictatorship

17: Two Cooperating Governments (Roll two more times)*

18: Two Antagonistic Governments (Roll two more times)*

19: No Government (May be true, or roll again to see what the real government is)

20: Hidden Government ("No one gets in to see the Wizard! Not no way, not no how!")

*If you get one of these results again on the follow-up roll, you can choose between re-rolling or making the government increasingly fractal and divided.

Town Alignments (d12)

Not all towns are nice places to be, and not all are what characters might consider "civilized." Cultural and philosophical differences from town to town could be minor or drastic; roll here to randomly find out what the outlook of the typical citizen is within this town.

Alignment	Description
1: Organized	The citizens in this town believe in organizing themselves against threats or crisis. They respond well, quickly, and in an orderly fashion to any problems that characters bring to their attention or cause.
2: Free-Spirited	The citizens in this town believe in letting individuals choose their own path. They avoid organizing any large-scale projects that require the cooperation of citizens against their will.
3: Tyrannical	Some manner of tyranny rules over the citizens of this town. Some may support or justify the tyranny and its effects, but others who are more targeted by the regime certainly chafe under it.
4: Brutal/Survivalist	The citizens of this town believe in survival of the fittest. They care for almost no rule of law but instead believe that might makes right. Characters will find that they might get to easily victimize the townsfolk, and be victimized by them in turn.
5: Progressive	The citizens of this town believe in advancing culture and civilization forward. They seek to build upon academic and philosophical foundations to develop new, better ways of living.
6: Utopian	The citizens of this town believe that they can turn their city into a perfect paradise unlike any other seen in the world. Whether they are correct or not, they have bought into this dream, which may harm or hurt them in the long run.
7: Isolationist	The citizens of this town believe in keeping to themselves and their own affairs. They are unlikely to involve themselves politically in anything outside of their ways; on a personal scale, most citizens mind their own business.
8: Selfish/Cutthroat	The citizens of this town believe in backstabbing each other to get ahead. Everyone is looking for the chance to one-up each other, but everyone is also paranoid and on the lookout for any perceived threats.
9: Anarchist	The citizens of this town believe in no rule of law at all. For some reason they have seen the dangers of power and would rather no organization control their individual actions. Characters should do well here!

Alignment	Description
10: Totalitarian	Every aspect of the citizens' lives is controlled by the governmental authority in this town. They are regimented into obedience, and if there is any dissatisfaction or thoughts of resistance, they are swiftly crushed.
11: Compassionate	The citizens of this town believe in caring for and looking after not just their own, but other noncitizens as well. They are extremely welcoming and take pity upon the misfortunes of others.
12: Just	The citizens of this town believe in looking out for the needs of the greater good. The government and townsfolk have a good working relationship; the government generally takes care of those who have fallen on bad luck, and the citizens respect and honor their benevolent rulers.

Leadership Quirks (d20)

Whether the town is led by a single politician or noble, or a larger body of individuals, its unique features and quirks will have a huge impact on the town and how it is ruled. Roll here to see what makes your town's government unique.

Leadership	Description
1: Corrupt	Hopelessly corrupt, with some other faction—a criminal element, a rival political power, or a secret individual—either blackmailing or bribing the government for power and influence.
2: Rigid	The inheritor of traditions and rites that go back hundreds, if not thousands of years, this government severely frowns upon changing or breaking with those traditions.
3: Severe	Extremely severe in executing justice upon criminals, enemies, and others who do not fall in line. The draconian laws are generally approved by the population, or they are too afraid to say otherwise.
4: High Taxes	Known for exacting especially high taxes, much to the disgust and anger of the townsfolk. The town itself is quite wealthy, but the citizens can easily be pushed to riot.
5: Low Taxes	Generally lax about collecting the little taxes they do levy, and plays a minor role in the lives of the townsfolk. In times of crisis, however, there are fewer communal resources to draw upon.
6: Religious Influences	Heavily influenced by a local deity, faith, or cult. This likely gives the religion a great deal of unspoken power within the town.
7: Foreign Influences	Under the influence of a foreign government, faction, or entity. The influence may be insidious, or merely seen as such by certain elements of the populace.
8: Ineffective	Completely incompetent at doing its job. This may be due to a foolish individual in power or a deliberately bloated system of rule that prevents any work from getting done.
9: Inexperienced	Either too young or too new to their position to rule effectively. Their intentions may be good, but their actions and proclamations often cause unexpected consequences.
10: Divided	A divided leadership causes conflict between the two political factions in town, and the division may take root in a third, separate faction looking to divide the town intentionally.

Leadership	Description
11: Scandalous	Seemingly always embroiled in one dramatic scandal after another. These scandals, while shocking, generally have no long-term political consequences—except the government's steadily dropping esteem in the eyes of the townsfolk.
12: Disintegrating	Steadily declining over time, and other rival factions are already circling in for the kill. It will not be long before the leadership collapses and a new one replaces it.
13: Familial	A single family, bloodline, or family-like cultural lineage dominates. It is difficult to get anywhere in town without being a member of the family, or at least paying them respect.
14: Bureaucratic	Enmeshed in a long-standing bureaucratic system of paperwork, stamps, clerks, political officials, signatures, and special permissions. It is not hard to get things done—for those who know how to work the system.
15: Expansionist	Focused on expanding the town's borders into the nearby wilderness or other occupied lands. This may be through military intervention, mass migration, or simply the natural population growth taking its toll.
16: Militaristic	Sees war as the solution to most of the town's problems, and constantly pushes the town and population in the direction of conflict with undesirable neighbors.
17: Imperialist	Desires to conquer neighboring lands and towns, rendering them vassals or colonies of the town. This may be a general impulse, or the town might have one clear target in mind.
18: Free Market	Believes ardently in letting merchants and businesses dictate their own needs and laws. They take a laissez-faire approach to the market.
19: Relaxed	Largely uninvolved in the affairs of the citizens and tends to take an "all's well" approach to every problem.
20: Magical Influences	Magical, supernatural forces control the town's leadership. The town, and indeed the leadership itself, might be blissfully unaware of this influence.

Town Guard Features (d20)

Whether quiet burg or a bustling metropolis, every town needs some individuals who are committed to keeping the public order. The town guard is there to ensure that law and order prevails, which means that the characters, in the natural way of things, will cause them some sort of grief at some point. Roll on this table to add features to individualize the guards of a particular town or district.

Town Guard	Description
1: Military	Consists almost entirely of professional soldiers from the local government's designated City Watch military branch. Depending on the nature of the local military, these guards may be strict or more lackadaisical with regard to law enforcement. In either case, they do take threats from outside of the town, especially foreign powers, extremely seriously.
2: Foreign	Made up of individuals from another country or kingdom, due to an invasion or change of power. They will probably be especially on edge and lash out at the local population with little provocation. The occupying forces do keep order and fight crime effectively; the nature of their role is at least somewhat benevolent, and likely even somewhat amicable.
3: Easygoing	Extremely friendly and helpful to adventurers, but otherwise lax in their duties. Characters with ill intent are more likely to get away with their crimes. They are just as likely, however, to be the targets of crime, or suffer other consequences of the town's ineffective security.
4: Progressive	More open-minded and accepting than elsewhere in the country or kingdom. They generally don't hold the same stereotypes about unusual races, beliefs, magics, or other lifestyles that other guards might hold against characters. This may be due to the general diversity of the guard itself, or the town, or the guard is making an intentional effort to let older ways of thinking die.
5: Draconian	Needlessly strict and authoritative, arresting citizens over technicalities and slight infractions. They may be subject to the will of a cruel or demented tyrant, who delights in tormenting their citizens (who are rendered criminals almost by default), or it may be the guards' way of shaking down citizens for money by extorting imaginary fines.
6: Lazy	Extremely reluctant to do their job. This may be due to low morale, low pay, rock-bottom recruiting standards, or a general lack of interest. Guards might be bribed or coerced into executing the law on the characters' behalf. At the same time, they will be reluctant to prosecute any crimes committed by the characters that do not directly threaten the local citizenry.

Town Guard	Description
7: Sparse	There are almost no guards in town. The citizens either police themselves effectively, or anarchy ensues. This is the sort of situation that can turn the characters into a party of warlords and robber-barons! But it is also likely that the characters are not the first group of well-armed individuals to attempt such a coup. Competition, in fact, might abound.
8: Xenophobic	Extremely unfriendly to foreigners, nontypical races and species, and/or outsiders in general. Such individuals are targeted unfairly, accused of crimes that they did not commit, and punished in excess of what others would receive for similar infractions. This attitude may reflect the town in general, or be unique to the guard.
9: Incompetent	Enthusiastic but woefully inept and routinely fails at their assigned tasks. Their bumbling is just as likely to cause problems for peaceful, law-abiding characters as it is to allow more chaotic individuals to get away with their crimes. They often show up in great numbers just to accent their utter inability en masse.
10: Zealous	Almost universally subscribes to a particular religion, philosophical code, oath, or cause that is either supportive or antagonistic of the governments' goals. Their beliefs lend a fanatical aura to all of their public work and their approach to violence in general. Some guards are tolerant of those outside of their order, but others show a clear disdain for those who hold different beliefs than their own.
11: Devoted	Utterly committed to a nonreligious cause of some kind, particular to the town. This cause might be political (the well-being of the local princess), economic (the protection of the mayor's orchards), or social (watching the monthly jousting tourney). Their enthusiasm might be coerced or sincere, but either way it clouds their vision and can cause them to make strategic mistakes.
12: Hardened	Numerous large-scale wars, dangers, and/or crime sprees have made the guard a powerful and seasoned force to be reckoned with. They do not take infractions against the law lightly, nor are they pushovers in combat, even against seasoned heroes. They may be strategically prepared for even the most unlikely attempts to circumvent their security measures.
13: Well-Equipped	Due to government funding, a wealthy patron, or other access to resources, the guard is especially well-equipped when compared to other militaries in the region. In addition to bearing the best arms and armor in the kingdom, the guard has access to other powerful weapons and forces, magical or otherwise.

Town Guard	Description
14: Underfunded	Does not have access to adequate resources to arm their troops properly, and some guards need to supply their own weapons. Characters may see a lot of improvised armor and weapons, or a lack of armaments entirely, on local guards. Guards may be jealous or easily bribed by how much easier the characters' equipment would make their lives.
15: Magically Enhanced	Uses magic in the course of carrying out their duties, either for combat, crime-solving, or other, less savory purposes. A spellcaster or a single individual who is the source of their magical abilities may be embedded amongst their ranks. The townsfolk might love or fear these powers.
16: Monstrous	Uses monstrous employees, captives, or pets in the course of its duty, perhaps for fighting or tracking down criminals. This relationship may hint at the monstrous nature of the guard themselves, or alternately, their comfort and familiarity in aggressively dealing with monsters and monstrous prisoners.
17: Cowardly	Capable, but fear grips them when combat breaks out. They are unwilling to risk their lives to save anyone but themselves. This can easily turn the guards into another set of potential victims (in addition to the other townsfolk they are supposed to be protecting) whenever danger should break out in town.
18: Broken	Whether they be benevolent or wicked, the ruling authorities in town are feared by the guard just as fiercely as they are by the ordinary townsfolk. This may be due to a supernatural power or control which the leadership exercises, or more mundane abuse of legal authority. In any case, the guard will never cross the authorities, and are likely to not be the true source of power in town.
19: Infiltrated	Political enemies, criminal elements, creepy cultists, or some other faction has worked spies, sleeper agents, or even disguised troops amongst the town guard. There is a (1d10 x 5)% chance that any given guard is secretly an enemy agent, working to either disrupt the guard, the town's leadership, or the characters themselves.
20: Adventurers	Whether due to their power level or thanks to sheer numbers, most of the policing in town is handled by a cast of quirky adventurers, not so different from the characters themselves. These rival adventurers may behave like heroic crime fighters or unpleasantly mirror the party's own behavior.

Unique City Defenses (d20)

Every town needs some sort of defenses, whether it's a single lookout or an entire series of defensive fortifications. Roll here to determine what unique features might set a town's defenses apart from the rest.

1: Fortified Temples/Monasteries

2: Free-Standing Archer Towers

3: Defensive Trebuchets

4: Secondary Walls

5: Deadfalls and Hidden Ditches

6: Secret Entrance/Exit

7: Constructed Traps

8: Defensive Ditches

9: Thick Crenellated Walls

10: Defensive Ballistae

11: Crude/Early Cannons

12: Defensive Catapults

13: Permanent Chevaux de Frise

14: Motte-and-Bailey Castle

15: Fortified Harbors

16: Moat and Drawbridge

17: Fortified City Gatehouse

18: Defensive Cliffs

19: Sally Port

20: Supernatural Guardian

Buildings (d100)

Not every building on every street corner needs to be fully fleshed out; but when the characters get up to their old tricks, it's helpful to find out what building or shop they just blew up, climbed, or attempted to rob. Roll here to generate random buildings in your town, adding to the roll in accordance with the quality of the local neighborhood.

Neighborhood Quality:

Impoverished: +0 | **Low:** +10 | **Average:** +20 | **High:** +30 | **Noble:** +40

1–6: Impoverished Residence

7–11: Impoverished Services (see page 31)

12–15: Impoverished Shop (see page 28)

16–17: Warehouse

18–19: Minor Shrine

20–21: Guardpost

22: Prison

23–28: Poor Residence

29–31: Low-Quality Restaurant

32–34: Low-Quality Services (see page 30)

35–37: Low-Quality Inn

38–41: Low-Quality Shop (see page 28)

42: Open-Air Market

43: Low-Quality Theater

44: Memorial

45: Graveyard

46–53: Average Residence

54–58: Average Restaurant

59–64: Average Services (see page 30)

65–73: Average Inn

74–85: Average Shop (see page 26)

86–87: Modest Church

88: Guard Barracks

89: Park

90–94: Upscale Residence

95–97: High-Quality Restaurant

98–100: High-Quality Services (see page 29)

101–103: High-Quality Inn

104–106: High-Quality Shop (see page 25)

107: Large Temple

108: Monument

109: Library

110: Guildhall

111: High-Quality Theater

112: Embassy

113: Diplomatic Residence

114: Bank

115: Servant House

116–120: Noble Estate

121: University

122: Mortuary

123: Dungeon

124: Mausoleum

125: Bureaucrat Offices

126: Sacred Green

127–130: Exotic Residence

131–132: Exotic Restaurant

133–134: Exotic Inn

135–136: Exotic Services (see page 28)

137–138: Exotic Shop (see page 25)

139: Grand Cathedral

140: Governmental Hall

Exotic Shops (d20)

1: Alchemist

2: Art Dealer

3: Calligrapher

4: Costumer

5: Sea Coral Dealer

6: Imported Goods Dealer

7: Magic Armor Dealer

8: Magic Item Dealer (General)

9: Magic Weapon Dealer

10: Pet Merchant

11: Potion Dealer

12: Rare Wood Merchant

13: Scroll Merchant

14: Soap Maker

15: Spice Merchant

16: Trapmaker

17: Wand Merchant

18: Exotic Clothier

19: Mapseller

20: Antique Dealer

High-Quality Shops (d20)

1: Perfumer

2: Bookbinder

3: Bookseller

4: Candy Maker

5: Clockmaker

6: Cosmetics Dealer

7: Curio Dealer

8: Dice Maker

9: Distiller

10: Draper

11: Toymaker

12: Fine Clothier

13: Gemcutter

14: Girdler

15: Glassblower

16: Glazier

17: Goldsmith

18: Inkmaker

19: Jeweler

20: Papermaker

Average Shops (d100)

1: Ale Merchant

2: Armorer

3: Baker

4: Bazaar Merchant

5: Beekeeper

6: Beer Merchant

7: Bellmaker

8: Blacksmith

9: Bonecarver

10: Bottler

11: Bowyer

12: Brandy Merchant

13: Brewer

14: Butcher

15: Buttonmaker

16: Cabinet Maker

17: Carpenter

18: Carpet Maker

19: Cartwright

20: Chainmaker

21: Chandler

22: Cheesemaker

23: Chemist

24: Clothier

25: Cobbler

26: Cooper

27: Coppersmith

28: Cutler

29: Dairy Merchant

30: Fletcher

31: Florist

32: Furniture Maker

33: Furrier

34: Glovemaker

35: Grocer

36: Haberdasher

37: Hardware Seller

38: Herbalist

39: High-Quality Fence/Dealer

40: Ivory Merchant

41: Joiner

42: Knifesmith

43: Lacemaker

44: Lampmaker

45: Leadworker

46: Locksmith

47: Luthier (Lutemaker)

48: Mason

49: Mead Merchant

50: Merchant (Trade goods)

51: Milliner

52: Music Dealer

53: Outfitter

54: Parchment Maker

55: Pastrycook

56: Pewterer

57: Playwright

58: Plumber/Dredger

59: Poet

60: Potter

61: Provisioner

62: Purse Maker

63: Quillmaker

64: Quilter

65: Religious Items Dealer

66: Roofer

67: Ropemaker

68: Rum Merchant

69: Saddler

70: Sailmaker

71: Salter

72: Scabbard Maker

73: Sculptor

74: Sealmaker

75: Seamstress

76: Shingler

77: Shipwright

78: Silk Merchant

79: Silversmith

80: Slave Trader

81: Stonecutter

82: Tailor

83: Tapestry Maker

84: Taxidermist

85: Thatcher

86: Threadmaker

87: Tilemaker

88: Tiler

89: Tinker

90: Tobacco Merchant

91: Vintner

92: Weaponsmith

93: Weaver

94: Wheelwright

95: Whipmaker

96: Wigmaker

97: Wiresmith

98: Wine Merchant

99: Woodworker

100: Writer

Low-Quality Shops (d20)

1: Bait and Tackle

2: Trinket Peddler

3: Brickmaker

4: Wool Merchant

5: Buckle Maker

6: Candlemaker

7: Tanner

8: Dyer

9: Thatcher

10: Fishmonger

11: Fuller

12: Hay Seller

13: Leatherworker

14: Livestock Merchant

15: Lumberer

16: Miller

17: Netmaker

18: Roofer

19: Rope Maker

20: Rug Maker

Impoverished Shops (d10)

1: Meat Pie Vendor

2: Pigeon Seller

3: Knickknack Peddler

4: Straw Seller

5: Stolen Goods Seller

6: Low-Quality Fence/Dealer

7: Firewood Seller

8: Charcoal Burner

9: Basket Weaver

10: Broommaker

Exotic Services (d10)

1: Astrologer

2: Historian

3: Master Storyteller

4: Bounty Hunter

5: Specialty Spellcaster for Hire

6: Masseur

7: Instrument Maker

8: Engineer

9: Mewskeeper

10: Kennel Master

High-Quality Services (d20)

1: Animal Trainer

2: Apothecary

3: Architect

4: Assassin

5: Auctioneer

6: Banker

7: Barrister

8: Cartographer

9: Professional Chef

10: Dentist

11: Engraver

12: Illuminator

13: Bookkeeper

14: Veterinarian

15: Sage

16: Scribe

17: Spellcaster for Hire

18: Translator

19: Tutor

20: Undertaker

Average Services (d20)

1: Teacher

2: Barber

3: Tattooer

4: Brothel Owner

5: Clerk

6: Cook

7: Fortuneteller

8: Freight Shipper

9: Gardener

10: Guide

11: Healer

12: Horse Trainer

13: Interpreter

14: Laundress

15: Mercenary

16: Messenger

17: Stable Owner

18: Moneychanger

19: Navigator

20: Painter

Low-Quality Services (d20)

1: Acrobat

2: Apprentice

3: Actor

4: Boater

5: Sellsword

6: Minstrel

7: Building Painter

8: Ship Painter

9: Carter

10: Bookie

11: Gambling Hall Owner

12: Teamster

13: Warehouse Owner

14: Low-Class Brothel Owner

15: Limner

16: Linkboy

17: Livestock Handler

18: Moneylender

19: Nursemaid

20: Pawnshop

Impoverished Services
(d12)

1: Beggar

2: Dangerous Brothel Owner

3: Rat Catcher

4: Thug for Hire

5: Dogfight Pitmaster

6: Wet Nurse

7: Buffoon

8: Juggler

9: Laborer

10: Porter

11: Shepherd

12: Burglar

General Structures (d100)

Sometimes it's not enough to know what a building is and who lives there; plans might require an accurate layout of one or more local buildings. Roll here to generate a random structural floorplan for the building in town. Add to the roll according to the wealth level of the building's district.

District Wealth:

Impoverished: +0 | **Low:** +10 | **Average:** +20 | **High:** +30 | **Noble:** +40

1-60: 1 story

61-70: 1 story, 1-floor basement

71-75: 1 story, 1-story tower/turret

76-80: 1 story, 1-floor basement, 1-story tower/turret

81-100: 2 stories

101-103: 2 stories, 1-floor basement

104-106: 2 stories, 1-story tower/turret

107: 2 stories, 2-floor basement

108: 2 stories, 2-story tower/turret

109: 2 stories, 1-floor basement, 1-story tower/turret

110: 2 stories, 1-floor basement, 2-story tower/turret

111-122: 3 stories

123: 3 stories, 1-floor basement

124: 3 stories, 1-story tower/turret

125: 3 stories, 2-floor basement

126: 3 stories, 2-story tower/turret

127: 3 stories, 1-floor basement, 1-story tower/turret

128: 3 stories, 1-floor basement, 2-story tower/turret

129: 3 stories, 2-floor basement, 1-story tower/turret

130: 3 stories, 2-floor basement, 2-story tower/turret

131: 4 stories

132: 4 stories, 1-floor basement

133: 4 stories, 1-story tower/turret

134: 4 stories, 2-floor basement

135: 4 stories, 2-story tower/turret

136: 4 stories, 1-floor basement, 1-story tower/turret

137: 4 stories, 1-floor basement, 2-story tower/turret

138: 4 stories, 2-floor basement, 1-story tower/turret

139: 4 stories, 2-floor basement, 2-story tower/turret

140: 5 stories, 3-floor basement, 2-story tower/turret

Interiors (d20)

Never judge a book by its cover—and likewise, never judge a building until you've seen it from the inside! The interior of a home, workplace, shop, or other structure can give ideas of the relative wealth of the occupants, or simply help to set a vivid scene indoors. Roll here to see what manner or style of interior you'll find upon walking into a particular building. Add the following modifier based on the quality of the local neighborhood:

Neighborhood quality:

Impoverished: +0 | **Low:** +1 | **Average:** +2 | **High:** +3 | **Noble:** +4

Interior	Description
1: Ramshackle	Has been allowed to fall into complete and utter disrepair. Major renovations need to be done to make this livable.
2: Shoddy	Was poorly crafted from the start; signs of shoddy work can be seen everywhere, by any halfway-decent craftsperson.
3: Sparse	Has few furnishings or decorations, and the owners have obviously kept their lifestyle simple out of financial necessity.
4: Spartan	Has been intentionally cleared of any decorations and furnishings other than the bare minimum. There may be many reasons for the owners to have made this choice.
5: Dirty	Livable, but the messy occupants have made it undesirable to live here. It needs a thorough cleaning to get the smell and stains out.
6: Damaged	Badly damaged by some ordinary, everyday accident, or else by some major event that occurred in the town's recent history. The space is still livable, but only just.
7: Weathered	Has withstood almost constant use by many hardworking, busy individuals. As such, while the interior might not be so old, it is worn and weathered by many feet and hands.
8: Aged	Has not been changed or updated in many generations, and the years have begun to show. Not only is the quality of the furnishings starting to give way, the style and aesthetics are utterly dated and maybe even antique.
9: Dusty	Has been kept in good repair, but is not frequently used or cleaned; as such, large quantities of dust and other signs of infrequent use (squeaky doors, etc.) are in evidence.
10: Modest	Has simple but nice accommodations for the area; nothing to brag about.

Interior	Description
11: Cozy	Fairly simple but has a lived-in, homey feel that suggests comfort. Roaring fires, comfortable chairs, and other nice furnishings are scattered about.
12: Rustic	Has a rustic feel, including hunting trophies and other signs of country living. Depending on where the structure is, this may be an entirely affected aesthetic on the owners' part.
13: Open	Can barely be considered "inside" at all; an open floor plan, such as either an open wall or ceiling, makes it feel open to the world, albeit exposed to the elements.
14: Windowed	Many windows (glass or open) allow large quantities of light inside. There is no need for candles or lamps here, at least during the day.
15: Spotless	Meticulously clean, dusted, and polished. There may even be sheets on the furniture!
16: New/ Renovated	Recently upgraded or built completely from scratch; everything is shiny and new.
17: Elegant	Reflects wealth, but does not include loud or ornate displays; instead, it is understated, simple, and suggests modesty on the owners' part.
18: Solid Crafting	Has sturdy furniture, solid foundations, and is difficult to damage.
19: Eccentric	Has unusual furnishings and conversation-starting decorations that heavily reflect upon the unique tastes of the owner.
20: Refined	High-quality, suggesting the expensive tastes of the owners while remaining classy and respectable and fancy, but not TOO fancy.
21: Baroque	Decorated like a work of art, with all of the furniture and architecture working to create the most aesthetically pleasing result.
22: Decadent	Signs of the opulent lifestyle and tastes of the owners are clearly visible. They spare no expense with decorations, regardless of how tasteless their displays of wealth are considered in town.
23: Gothic	Old, ornate, and moody to the point of being spooky. It's obviously expensive, but far from cozy.
24: Supernatural	Somehow defies the traditional limitations of either space (bigger on the inside), time (ageless furniture), or decoration (supernatural materials).

Decor (d20)

Even the most modest home or structure might have decorations scattered about. Whether they will be used as improvised weapons or the party plans to case the joint, roll here to see what decor is present in a given location.

Decor	Description
1: Hanging Plants	Flowers, vines, or other plants hang all around, either climbing up the walls or in pots hanging from the ceiling.
2: Pedestal	A beautiful central pedestal or several rows of pedestals decorate this room. They may have other decorations mounted atop them; roll again to see what, if anything, adorns them.
3: Statue	A statue here depicts a humanoid or other creature of importance or fame within the community. The subject of the statue has extra importance at this location.
4: Sculpture	A sculpture here depicts a symbol, place, or abstract idea. It represents something of great importance to the people at this location.
5: Tree	Whether outdoors or indoors with a modified roof to allow it to grow, there is a living tree at this location. It may be considered important for other reasons, but this living decoration is nothing if not irreplaceable.
6: Potted Plant	One or more potted plants fill the floor of this area with a distinctive and refreshing natural atmosphere.
7: Candlesticks	Candles and candlesticks/sconces fill this location, lighting the way for residents to walk about. They offer romantic lighting and a ready source of flame.
8: Lamps	This location is filled with working oil-burning lamps that illuminate the room. They provide lovely ambiance, as well as ammunition in a pinch.
9: Fountain	An appropriately sized central fountain dominates this location. It may still be active and working, spouting water from the mouth of some mythical beast (see page 123), or it may have run dry long ago.
10: Thick Carpets	A vast central carpet or several smaller rugs decorate this location. They might have beautiful patterns or be made of especially fine, soft material.
11: Pillows	A large central pillow, or an assortment of multicolored pillows, are scattered around this location. These pillows can be used as seats for guests or to make one amazing fort.
12: Musical Instruments	One large musical instrument or a variety of musical instruments are mounted on the walls or occupy the floor space of this location (see page 139).

Decor	Description
13: Urn/Vase	A large vase or urn, or an arrangement of such ceramic works, decorates this location. They may be empty and decorative or hold sentimental items (such as family ashes/remains).
14: Stained Glass	A series of stained glass windows, possibly including one massive central window, depict historical and/or religious scenes throughout this location.
15: Mounted Animal Head	One large stuffed animal, or a variety of mounted animal heads, are mounted on the walls or occupy the floor space of this location (see page 166).
16: Portrait Drawing	A portrait, or several portraits, have been drawn and hung at this location. The individuals depicted might be the residents, family members, or people of importance to the location.
17: Portrait Painting	A portrait, or several portraits, have been painted and hung at this location. The individuals depicted might be the residents, family members, or people of importance to the location.
18: Landscape Painting	A depiction of a natural vista has been painted and hung at this location. The view being depicted might be a nearby place, or somewhere of importance to this location.
19: Glass Sculpture	This location is decorated by a sculpture not of stone, but glass. Much more valuable and precious, but also much, much more vulnerable and delicate!
20: Monument	This location features a monument to a famous war, event, or person in history. This may simply be a plaque or a dedication/carving on the wall or door; otherwise, roll again to see what physical form the monument takes.

Walls (d20)

Not every wall will survive a fiery explosion—some won't even survive a punch! Roll here to see what material the walls of a particular structure are made out of. Add to the roll according to the wealth level of the building's district.

District Wealth:
Impoverished: +0 | **Low:** +1 | **Average:** +2 | **High:** +3 | **Noble:** +4

1-4: Mud/Earth

5: Thatched

6-7: Wattle & Daub

8-12: Wood

13-18: Stone

19-22: Bricks

23-24: Marble/Granite

Floors (d20)

Whether you are digging into the local bank or smashing down into a tavern basement, a well-constructed floor could be the difference between life and death. Roll here to see what material the floor of a particular structure is made out of. Add to the roll according to the wealth level of the building's district.

District Wealth:
Impoverished: +0 | **Low:** +1 | **Average:** +2 | **High:** +3 | **Noble:** +4

1-2: Leaves/Grass

3-4: Mud/Earth

5-7: Straw

8-10: Loose Wooden Boards & Sawdust

11-13: Loose Wooden Boards

14-16: Firm Wooden Boards

17-22: Stone

23-24: Marble/Granite

Rooftops (d20)

Leaping from rooftop to rooftop might be a quick and heroic-looking way to travel around, but its effectiveness largely depends on the quality of the roof being traversed. Roll here to determine the predominant roofing material of a certain town, or to throw a "surprise" roof at a character making a blind jump.

1: Leaves/Grass

2-3: Mud/Earth

3-5: Thatched

6-9: Wattle & Daub

10: Weatherproof Skins/Leathers

11: Wooden Boards

12: Wooden Shingles

13: Slate Tiles

14: Stone

15-16: Bricks

17: Iron Shingles

18-19: Plaster/Mortar

20: Marble/Granite

Understory Walls & Floors (d20)

A basement level needs to be secure, dry, and safe. Roll here to see what material the basement floor of a particular structure is made out of. Add to the roll according to the wealth level of the building's district.

District Wealth:
Impoverished: +0 | **Low:** +1 | **Average:** +2 | **High:** +3 | **Noble:** +4

1–4: Earth/Dirt

5: Wattle & Daub

6–9: Loose Wooden Boards

10–14: Firm Wooden Boards

15–19: Stone

20–22: Bricks

23–24: Marble/Granite

Sublevels (d20)

Beneath the buildings in town, beneath even the basements and vaults, there may be a thriving underworld. Roll here to see what manner of sublevel is found beneath the basement level of a particular building, or below the town in general. Add to the roll according to the size of the town.

Town Size:
Hamlet: +0 | **Village:** +2 | **Town:** +4 | **Small City:** +6 | **Large City:** +8 | **Metropolis:** +10

1–13: No Sublevel

14: Subterranean Cemetery

15–16: Smuggler Tunnels

17–19: Transport Tunnels

20: Mine Tunnels

21–22: Connected Cellars

23–25: Low-Quality Sewers

26–28: High-Quality Sewers

29: Modern Catacombs

30: Ancient Catacombs

Terrain (d20)

Towns don't exist in empty space; the land where people build their homes was once wilderness of some kind. The land outside of town might still be that same terrain, or different terrain. Roll here to see what kind of terrain lies beneath, or around, town.

1: Grassland

2: Plain

3: Prairie

4: Hills

5: Mountain

6: Forest

7: Lake

8: Scrubland

9: Shore

10: Valley

11: Rocky Badlands

12: Canyon

13: Swamp

14: Marsh

15: River

16: Steppe

17: Oasis

18: Desert

19: Tundra

20: Arctic

Crops (d20)

All towns need farms and farmland to feed their hungry populations—it's just a matter of how far those farms are from city limits. Once you reach the edges of town, roll here to see what local crops are growing in the local vicinity, or to see what crops the town's farmers might focus on.

1: Barley

2: Wheat

3: Oats

4: Rye

5: Olives

6: Spinach

7: Cabbages

8: Beans

9: Peas

10: Onions

11: Potatoes

12: Apple Trees

13: Pear Trees

14: Turnips

15: Rice

16: Citrus Fruit Trees (Oranges, Limes, or Lemons)

17: Aubergine

18: Sugar Cane

19: Cotton

20: Spices (Cinnamon, Nutmeg, or Coriander)

Seasons (d4)

The current season can make a major impact on what is happening in a given city. Harvests, holidays, and weather can all depend on what time of the year it is. If it becomes relevant to know what season it is, roll here to randomize it.

1: Spring

2: Summer

3: Fall

4: Winter

Climates (d20)

Weather changes, but every town has a typical climate to which they can expect the weather to roughly adhere. Roll here to generate a random climate for your city, a region or kingdom, or even for your entire fantasy setting.

1-2: Tropical (Very Hot & Wet)

3-5: Humid (Hot & Wet)

6: Desert (Hot & Dry)

7-13: Mild

14-17: Damp (Cold & Wet)

18-19: Tundra (Cold & Dry)

20: Arctic (Very Cold & Dry)

Weather (d20)

Sometimes it becomes important to know what the weather is in town, for the purposes of fights, chase scenes, or just for scenery dressing. While this table might not be a statistically accurate representation of the region's climate, rolling here gives a selection of interesting weather patterns to make any outdoor scene more exciting.

1: Rain

2: Downpour

3: Cold

4: Warm

5: Hot

6: Freezing

7: Thunderstorm

8: Fog

9: Snow

10: Heavy Snow

11: Blustery

12: Heavy Winds

13: Breezy

14: Sleet

15: Hail

16: Duststorm/Sandstorm

17: Clear

18: Cloudy

19: Misty

20: Disaster Weather (see page 45)

Natural Disasters (d20)

Sometimes a Game Master needs to call in a disaster and it doesn't matter what kind. How did that old tower get destroyed? What killed the farming families south of town, causing the recent influx of refugees? What kind of punishment will a god send for sacrilege against their temple or holy site? Roll here to generate all manner of environmental catastrophes.

1: Severe Heat Wave

2: Blight

3: Drought

4: Tsunami

5: Flood

6: Hailstorm

7: Hurricane

8: Heavy Fog

9: Meteorite Impact

10: Blizzard

11: Lightning Storm

12: Typhoon

13: Environmental Pollution

14: Earthquake

15: Wildfire

16: Pestilence

17: Avalanche

18: Mudslide

19: Tornado

20: Supernatural Plague

Illnesses, Maladies, and Plagues (d20)

Sometimes a corpse or townsperson's sad backstory needs to get fleshed out, or a certain crime warrants a divine-level punishment. Roll here to generate the sort of diseases that might break out in a town (especially a town with adventurers returning to sell potentially infected loot).

1: Blindness

2: Measles

3: "St. Anthony's Fire"/Skin Rash

4: Cholera

5: Gout

6: Tuberculosis

7: Syphilis

8: Deformities

9: Common Cold/Flu

10: Dysentery

11: Arthritis

12: Unnatural Madness

13: Black Death/Bubonic Plague

14: Mental Illness

15: Fever

16: Chickenpox

17: Lice

18: Wound/Battlefield Infections

19: Leprosy

20: Magical Malady/Curse

Cures/Remedies (d20)

Medieval cures were not always pretty, enjoyable, or effective. While supernatural healing might get great mileage in your world, feel free to make any of these results turn out to be quack remedies. Roll here to determine the methods of a particular healer, the predominant healing techniques of a certain town, or the only known cure for a particular ailment.

1: Potion/Brew

2: Poultice

3: Bloodletting/Leeches

4: Prayers

5: Magic Stone/Charm

6: Soothing Ointments

7: Anointing Oils

8: Crystals/Precious Stones

9: Astrological Readings

10: Amputation

11: Therapeutic Bath

12: Edible Remedy (Garlic, ginger root, magic apple)

13: Stretching/Body Manipulation

14: Animal-Based Cure (Snails, urine, cat guts, etc.)

15: Acupuncture

16: Rudimentary Surgery

17: Quarantine/Isolation

18: Treated Bandages

19: Meditative Spiritwork

20: Hallucinogenic Spirit Journey

Legal Punishments (d100)

Some characters love to break the law, but few are enthusiastic about what comes after such incidents. Still, there's no fun to chaos without the threat of some juicy consequences! Roll here to generate a random legal punishment, adding to the roll in accordance with the severity of the crime.

Severity:

Minor Violation: +0 | **Small Misdemeanor:** +10 | **Lesser Felony:** +20 |
Moderate Felony: +30 | **Serious Felony:** +40 | **Unspeakable Crimes:** +50

1: Easy Warning

2: Stern Warning

3: Long, Stern Lecture

4: "Citation" (No effect)

5: Community Service (Short term)

6: Verbal Apology

7: Petty Fine/Tithe

8: Short Stay in the Stocks

9: Under Personal Watch

10: Imprisonment (Very brief)

11: Written Apology

12: Community Service (Long term)

13: Hat of Shame

14: Publicly Denounced

15: Minor Fine/Tithe

16: Minor Ordeal (Pluck a stone from a boiling pot)

17: Mask of Shame

18: Repentance Cloak

19: Minor Lashing/Flogging

20: Force Fasting

21: Exile/Banishment (Months/seasons)

22: Indentured Servitude (Months/seasons)

23: Force-Feeding

24: Public Humiliation

25: Imprisonment (Short)

26: Paraded around Town

27: Moderate Fine/Tithe

28: Trip in the Iron Cage

29: Long Stay in the Stocks

30: Tarred and Feathered

31: Shrew's Fiddle

32: Minor Edict

33: Moderate Ordeal (Holding a Burning Coal)

34: Minor Psychological Torture

35: Imprisonment (Medium)

36: Moderate Lashing/Flogging

37: Exile/Banishment (Years)

38: Bridle/Mask

39: Forced Labor

40: Religious Confinement

41: Forced Military Service

42: Toe Removal

43: Severe Fine/Tithe

44: Indentured Servitude (Years)

45: Barrel Pillory

46: Exposed to the Elements

47: Water Torture

48: Foot Whipping

49: Sisyphean Assignment

50: Finger Removal

51: Severe Lashing/Flogging

52: Imprisonment (Long term)

53: Moderate Edict

54: Exposed to Bees/Insects/Vermin

55: Branding

56: Thumbscrews

57: Cat o' Nine Tails

58: Exile/Banishment (Decades)

59: Iron Shoe

60: Teeth Removal

61: Tattooing

62: Extreme Fine/Tithe

63: Denailing

64: Bed of Nails

65: Indentured Servitude (Decades)

66: Foot Roasting

67: Moderate Psychological Torture

68: Iron Chair

69: Severe Ordeal (Walking across a bed of hot coals)

70: The Rack

71: Extremely Severe Edict

72: Imprisonment (Lifetime)

73: Disfigurement

74: Strappado

75: Excommunication

76: King's Ransom Fine/Tithe

77: Brodequins

78: Forfeiture of All Property

79: Exile/Banishment (Lifetime)

80: Trial by Combat

81: Hand Removal

82: Tongue Removal

83: Eye Removal

84: Foot Removal

85: Castration

86: Both Hands Removed

87: Full Blinding

88: Dunking

89: Confined Isolation

90: Hemlock Poisoning

91: Beheading

92: Hanging

93: Guillotine

94: Defenestration

95: Smothered in Ash

96: Thrown off a Cliff

97: Stoning

98: Drowning

99: Disembowelment

100: Execution by Weapon

101: Slavery (Lifetime)

102: Severe Psychological Torture

103: Trampled by Animals

104: Keelhauling

105: Death by Dehydration

106: Dismemberment

107: Knee Splitter

108: Death by Starvation

109: Pendulum

110: Buried Alive

111: Impalement

112: Manually Quartered

113: Wooden Horse

114: Lead Sprinkler

115: Catherine Wheel

116: Spanish Boot

117: Dipped in Boiling Water

118: Iron Maiden

119: Pear of Anguish

120: Burned Alive

121: Suffocation under Mud

122: Breast Ripper/Iron Spider

123: Dipped in Boiling Oil

124: Devoured by Rats

125: Thrown to Hungry Dogs

126: Heretic's Fork

127: Garotting

128: Thrown to "The Beast"

129: Headcrusher

130: Drawn and Quartered

131: Death by Sawing

132: Crushed by Stones

133: Hung until Near Death (Roll again for follow-up punishment)

134: Exquisitely Designed Psychological Torture

135: Flaying

136: Judas Cradle/Chair

137: Crocodile Tube

138: Blood Eagled

139: Intestinal Crank

140: Family Members Punished (Roll again for punishment)

141: Scavenger's Daughter

142: Gibbeting

143: Death by a Thousand Cuts

144: Coffin Torture

145: Brazen Bull

146: Drug-Induced Torture

147: Scaphism

148: Crucifixion

149: Magical/Supernatural Psychological Torture

150: Offered up to Divine Judgment (???)

Holidays (d20)

Traditional major holidays occur in most towns and communities. If the adventurers need the cover of an upcoming celebration or simply want to kick back and party, roll here to generate your own holidays for any time of the year!

Holiday	Description
1: Noble Nuptials	Celebrates the wedding of two local nobles, perhaps even members of a royal family. The wedding may have political implications, and the festivities end abruptly if anything goes wrong (or seems to).
2: Harvest Holiday	Celebrates the beginning of the harvest and the work that comes with it. Farmers and just about everyone else in town are busy with not only the fieldwork and the work of associated industries, but the festivities and long-held traditions that accompany the day.
3: Feast Holiday	Celebrates the successful completion of the harvest and the beginning of the harvest feasts. The communal feasts held throughout town offer some of the best and most plentiful fare of food and drinks to be had.
4: Fool's Holiday	Celebrates horror in a fun-loving way. Children dress up as monsters and run throughout town scaring each other and adults. Those who refuse them treats or coins will be made into their fool for the night and pranked without mercy.
5: Penance Holiday	This holiday may or may not have religious implications, but it does involve voicing one's sins and mistakes. Grievances might be brought up by the aggrieved, or each person might be responsible for confessing to each other—or perhaps even publicly!
6: Topsy-Turvy Holiday	A celebration of all things silly and mischievous. The king is fool for a day, the fool is king for a day, and everyone gets a big social catharsis out of getting to tell each other off and not have to face the consequences the next day.
7: Memorial Holiday	A memorial to a famous battle, foundation, birth, death, or discovery within the town's past. Re-creations of the famed event and stories of the town's history abound during this holiday, as the community collectively shores up its shared cultural narrative.
8: National Holiday	Dedicated to the nation, kingdom, or rulership under which the town falls, this holiday is intended as a patriotic celebration, including military demonstrations and revelry, but may bring up unpleasant political issues within the community.

Holiday	Description
9: Lover's Holiday	Celebrates love in all of its forms. Couples and would-be lovers exchange vows and plan special dates, while the prices of flowers and small token gifts skyrocket throughout the town.
10: Gift-Giving Day	A celebration of generosity in which townsfolk bestow gifts and blessings upon each other as signs of affection and love. The gifts may be exchanged openly or secretly as part of a playful holiday game.
11: Healing Day	May take place on the anniversary of a divine miracle or vision, or on a special feast day dedicated to a deity of life and healing. It is said that healing magic is especially powerful on this day, and those who ask for a miraculous cure may find their prayers answered.
12: The Trials	Celebrates competitions and tournaments of all sorts, some violent, some merely physical, and others more abstract (riddle games, etc.) or magical. The centerpiece of the day is a series of trials that a limited number of competitors in town are allowed to participate in.
13: Seasonal Holiday	Celebrates the midpoint of a particular season—if not with calendar accuracy, it at least embodies the spirit of the season. If you have not established the current season, generate it randomly (roll on page 43).
14: Effigy Holiday	Involves ceremonial burning of an effigy as the centerpiece of the festival. This effigy might be symbolic of the harvest season, the collective evil or darkness of the community, or of a particularly hated individual in the town's past.
15: Hero's Holiday	Dedicated to a particular hero, king, or other figure of fame and respect. The tenets which this individual upheld are spoken of and practiced today by most people in town who wish to honor the hero's memory.
16: Tax Holiday	Either when the official taxes are collected by the kingdom or government, or when an additional, smaller tax is collected for some official (but likely unpopular) reason. This tax certainly puts a damper on the day, making this a highly unpopular holiday.
17: Veteran's Holiday	Celebrates the town's armed forces, both today and in the past. It is usually accompanied by military demonstrations and other shows of respect and force, in which old former soldiers are honored.
18: Ancestor's Holiday	Celebrates the members of the town community who have passed away. Townsfolk put up household shrines to their lost ancestors and celebrate the life and death of those who came before.

Holiday	Description
19: Large Holiday	A holiday of particular importance to the town. Roll two times on this table to generate two unique features that describe this holiday, re-rolling any 19–20 results.
20: Major Holiday	A major aspect of the town's identity, possibly serving as the hub of their calendar year. Roll three times on this table to generate three unique features that describe this holiday, re-rolling any 19–20 results.

Strange Locations (d20)

Most towns have their share of strange and unusual locations that draw the attention, rumors, and romantic notions of the populace. Whether these locations are actually places of power or not is up to you. Roll here to see what interesting locale an adventurer stumbles across or hears about through local rumors.

Strange Location	Description
1: Weeping Statue	This statue is ordinary, except that at certain times it is said to cry tears of saltwater (or blood). These may be at random moments, during regular seasonal/holiday intervals, or during certain major historical incidents.
2: Haunted House	This house has been left abandoned for longer than many can remember. There is said to be a ghost, although the true horror of what lies in the basement may be far worse.
3: Moonlit Street	This hidden street or alley seems to cause strange effects upon the people who live and walk near it, such as madness and visions. Light seems to bend strangely in this place.
4: Enchanted Fountain	This fountain in the city may or may not have run dry; either way, it is purported to have magical properties. The magic may be a legend or may only work at certain times.
5: Bizarre Greenhouse	An indoor explosion of life is hidden in the midst of the town, thanks to the wonders of glass and architecture. The owner may have a particular reason for growing secret plants in the middle of town or may simply keep this place for recreation.
6: Hidden Ecosystem	A strangely vibrant ecosystem of thriving flora and fauna can be found here, somehow surprisingly healthy for the climate and conditions in which they are growing.
7: Secret Church	A secret meeting place for a religious group has been secreted away here—perhaps in plain sight. The group may be outlawed or frowned upon, perhaps with good reason.
8: Wax Sculpture Museum	This home or shop includes, as a side project, a wax sculpture museum of different creatures, individuals, or other more obscure subjects. Whether mundane or supernatural, the sculptures are eerie to behold.
9: Abandoned Tower	This tower is generally unoccupied, largely due to doubts (founded or unfounded) regarding its structural instability. Other, less particular occupants may have moved in as a result.

Strange Location	Description
10: Small Theater	A small run-down theater or open-air act with a strange group of performers with an uncanny edge, who might be locals, or just passing through.
11: Ancient Well	This well's origins are lost somewhere in the town's earliest histories. There may be unusual flora or fauna, or an ancient item buried somewhere in the depths.
12: Forgotten Cemetery	This cemetery has been forgotten, either because the family has left or died off, or because it was first built in secrecy.
13: Historical Landmark	A particular relic, monument, ruin, or ancient structure is on display here as a landmark commemorating the history of the town. No one is responsible for protecting it per se, but everyone will be disgruntled if something were to happen to it.
14: Grandmother Tree	This tree is a particularly old example of its species and reputedly was the progenitor of many of the younger trees around town. Local spiritual individuals hold it in high regard.
15: Secret Hideout	This small clubhouse, attic, or cellar serves as a meeting place or storage location for a group of secretive individuals in town. Their reasons for secrecy might be benign or insidious.
16: War Memorial	This large statue, pedestal, or stone commemorates a war and the soldiers who fought it. It may attract veterans, widows, and the restless spirits of fallen soldiers.
17: Foundational Stone	This ordinary-looking stone is held in reverence, perhaps even placed in a shrine of honor. It is claimed to be the foundational stone of the city, or where a famous founding leader first stood, was crowned, or claimed power in some manner.
18: Mythic Resting Place	This place has a small, innocuous marker, grave, or even just a carving that signifies that the remains of a famous hero or town leader are buried somewhere below (or at least nearby). The grave might be false, but the locals don't care.
19: Mystery Door	There is a door here that no one knows how to open, nor where it goes. The door will only open for the right person at the right time.
20: Lost Shrine	This shrine is dedicated to a god or cult that may no longer exist or has gone underground to hide. Roll to see what deity (see page 120) or cult (see page 118) the shrine might be dedicated to.

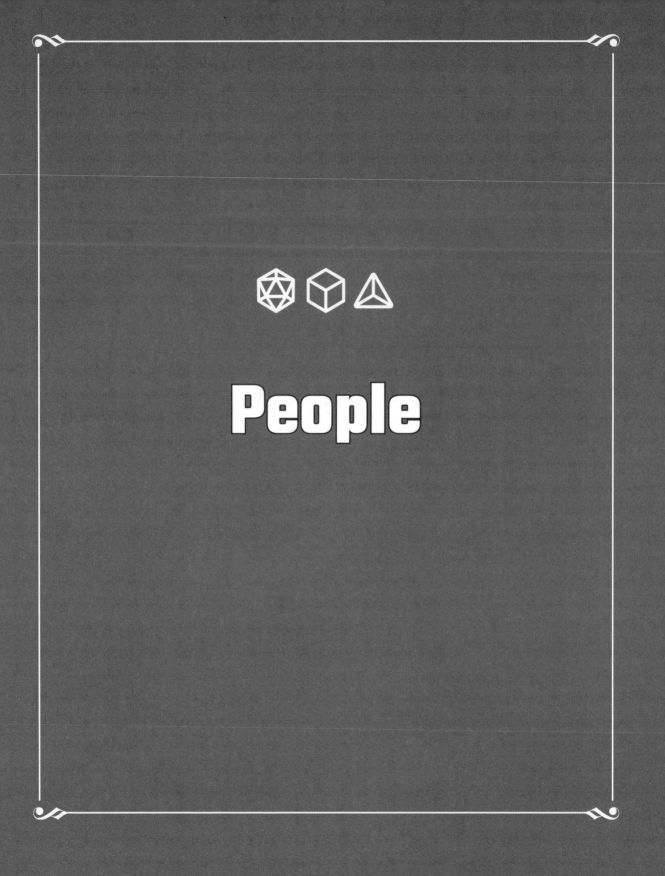

People

Moods (d100)

A random townsperson being accosted by a character has probably already had a long day. Roll here to find out what kind of mood a given person is in.

1: Friendly

2: Slow

3: Jolly

4: Impatient

5: Frugal

6: Furious

7: Adventurous

8: Foolhardy

9: Strong

10: Generous

11: Helpful

12: Patronizing

13: Taciturn

14: Gruff

15: Suspicious

16: Xenophobic

17: Knowledgeable

18: Wise

20: Playful

21: Eccentric

22: Anxious

23: Naughty

24: Stubborn

25: Sensitive

26: Nice

27: Emotional

28: Bad-Tempered

29: Nervous

30: Mean

31: Distracted

32: Dishonest

33: Rude

34: Discreet

35: Crazy

36: Cheeky

37: Cheerful

38: Energetic

39: Pessimistic

40: Optimistic

41: Unpleasant

42: Talkative

43: Calm

44: Passionate

45: Proud

46: Sincere

47: Lazy

48: Lively

49: Funny

50: Silly

51: Shy

52: Determined

53: Versatile

54: Sociable

55: Worried

56: Thoughtful

57: Humble

58: Frank

59: Obedient

60: Honest

61: Fearless

62: Unfriendly

63: Generous

64: Compassionate

65: Disobedient

66: Selfish

67: Imaginative

68: Placid

69: Jealous

70: Helpful

71: Enthusiastic

72: Persistent

73: Sensible

74: Self-Confident

75: Bossy

76: Plucky

77: Patient

78: Easygoing

79: Messy

80: Hard-Working

81: Kind

82: Loyal

83: Confident

84: Attentive

85: Scared

86: Gentle

87: Dynamic

88: Fair-Minded

89: Supportive

90: Timid

91: Brave

92: Ambitious

93: Happy

94: Romantic

95: Diplomatic

96: Courteous

97: Humorous

98: Self-Disciplined

99: Serious

100: Tidy

Local Gossip & Rumors (d20)

Lounging at the bar is likely to turn up more than a few rumors, especially for adventurers who are attentive to the local gossip. Roll here to see what scuttlebutt is being talked about in town, either by a particular individual or the majority.

Rumor	Description
1: Bridge Monster	A dangerous monster has made the river below a local bridge its domain. It is exacting tolls or outright devouring travelers who cross its way.
2: Serial Killer	A notorious murderer is on the loose, who has a signature killing style. No one knows where or when they will strike next, but it's possible to guess who the victim might be.
3: Road Danger	A problem is afflicting a local nearby road. It might be traffic issues, uncrossable terrain, or bandits on the road, but it's making getting into and out of town difficult.
4: Heavenly Sighting	Many (or all) of the locals have seen a vision in the sky: a comet, a star, an aurora, a mysterious face or image, or unusual clouds. It is not necessarily supernatural, but the locals seem to think it is.
5: New Industry	Some new industry has arrived in town, or an old dying industry has been restored to life. The benefits and prosperity are visible to everyone, so there is much to celebrate.
6: Wanted Fugitive	An individual who is wanted, either by the authorities or by the criminal elements (or both), is loose in town . Everyone knows the fugitive is in town, but no one knows exactly where. The details on their crime are hazy.
7: Rural Danger	A danger in the nearby area, such as bandits, monsters, or a rogue magic-user, has threatened farms and villages on the outskirts of town. This danger is far enough away that it is treated as an inconvenience, rather than a danger, by the townsfolk.
8: Upcoming Holiday	The town is talking about an upcoming holiday (roll on page 52). The circumstances of the holiday may have garnered extra attention; or, the town traditionally holds the upcoming holiday in high esteem.
9: Self-Inflicted Rumors	The ears of the adventurers must be burning, because THEY are the ones being gossiped about right now. The locals have learned of the party's exploits—which are hopefully good—and are discussing them, possibly right in front of their stories' protagonists!
10: Strange Visitor	A figure of power and mystery has entered town recently, and the town is talking about who exactly they are. People have theories, but no one knows for sure. (See page 78.)

Rumor	Description
11: Local Danger	A dangerous situation in the town itself, such as threatening individuals, powerful factions, or monstrous infiltrators have become hazardous to certain townsfolk. The problem is contained enough that not everyone is concerned, but there is a danger for those who get involved.
12: Seasonal Change	The town is talking about the upcoming seasonal shift and the implications it will have for trade, crops, and larger politics. If you have not established the current season, generate it randomly (roll on page 43).
13: Weather Hazard	The town is discussing the weather, and unfortunately, it's not all good news. Dangerous, perhaps even supernatural, weather patterns have forced inhabitants out of some regions or made routes near town impassable.
14: Local Villains	The town is talking about a local villain, or a group of villains. The villains may have just arrived in town or pulled off some successful heist or mission. Randomly generate villains as needed (roll on page 108).
15: Local Crimes	Local robberies, kidnappings, or other crimes have been afflicting the population. This crime may be new or particularly problematic at the moment. Randomly generate a criminal type if you need one (roll on page 105).
16: Guest Celebrity	A famous artisan, noble, or other celebrity has arrived in town recently, and the town is abuzz with excited fans. They will defend their hero excessively, especially if it is a controversial figure.
17: Faraway War	Events have transpired in a war far away from the town, which the townsfolk may or may not be invested in. Either way, the news is serious or interesting enough that rumors have reached town.
18: Brewing War	Rumors of a growing war have the townsfolk concerned over what will happen to their livelihood, and whether they will be drafted as soldiers.
19: Quest	A quest or mission—slaying a nearby monster or warlord, rescuing a local noble, retrieving a missing item—either needs to be completed or has just recently been completed to the town's delight.
20: Item of Legend	The town is talking about an item so famous and/or powerful that it is known in legend around the world.

Random Bystanders (d20)

Most towns have more people than your characters will likely ever meet. However, if they decide to scan the town square, go on a murder spree, or simply approach a random face on the street, it may be important to know who is standing around. Roll here to generate random citizens for street scenes and major setpiece battles. First, decide the wealth level of the district the characters are in, and then roll, referring to the appropriate column.

	Impoverished	Low	Average	High	Noble
Criminals & Troublemakers (page 65)	1–3	1–2	1	1	1
Townsfolk & Commoners (page 65)	4–7	3–9	2–9	2–7	2–6
Animals & Livestock (page 68)	8–10	10–11	10–11	8	7
Guards & Heroes (page 69)	11–12	12–13	12	9	8–9
Traffic & Hazards (page 68)	13–14	14–15	13	10	10
Priests & Preachers (page 70)	15–16	16	14	11	11
Merchants & Businessfolk (page 71)	17	17	15–16	12–13	12–14
Messengers & Speakers (page 72)	18	18	17	14–15	15–16
Performers & Entertainers (page 70)	19	19	18–19	16–17	17–18
Nobles & Royals (page 72)	20	20	19–20	18–20	17–20

Criminals & Troublemakers (d20)

1: Thief Disguised as a Beggar

2: Thief Disguised as a Townsperson

3: Thief Disguised as a Noble

4: Suspicious Individual Watching a Noble's Residence

5: Suspicious Individual Lurking at the Corner

6: Mysterious Carriage with Drawn Curtains

7: Foreign Assassin out on a Mission

8: 2 Suspicious Men Making a Secret Transaction

9: 1d4 Troublemaker Ruffians

10: Team of 1d4 Pickpockets

11: 1d4 Thieves Attempting to Scale a Wall

12: 1d6 Young Toughs Hanging Out

13: 1d6 Muggers

14: 2d4 Troublemaker Ruffians

15: Crew of 2d4 Pickpockets

16: 1d8 Thieves Attempting to Rob a Home

17: 2d6 Young Toughs Hanging Out

18: 2d8 Thieves Attempting to Rob a Building

19: Gang of 3d4 Pickpockets

20: Large Gang of 4d4 Thieves and Thugs

Townsfolk & Commoners (d100)

1: 1d4 Young Children Playing

2: 1d4 Children Playing

3: 2d6 Children Playing

4: 2d10 Children Playing

5: 1d4 Children Writing Graffiti on a Wall

6: 1d6 Children Playing with 1d4 Dogs

7: 1 Beggar

8: 1 Beggar Child

9: 1 Beggar and Dog

10: 1d2+1 Fishwives Arguing

11: 2d4 Fishwives Gossiping

12: 2d6 Fishwives Gossiping

13: 1 Indentured Porter Carrying Supplies

14: 1d6 Teamsters Unloading a Wagon

15: 2d4 Porters Carrying Supplies

16: 2d4 Porters (Empty-Handed)

17: 1d6 Bearers Carrying Large Cloth Loads

18: 1 Innocent Loitering Bystander

19: 2d4 Innocent Loitering Bystanders

20: 2d8 Innocent Loitering Bystanders

21: 1 Concerned, Helpful Citizen

22: 1d8 Concerned, Helpful Citizens

23: 1d8 Drunk Bystanders on Their Way Home

24: 1 Lone Horseman

25: 1 Lone horseman, Hood Pulled over His Head

26: 1 Wagondriver Making Deliveries

27: 1 Wagondriver Leaving Town

28: 1 Townsperson Arguing with Merchant over Freshness of Produce

29: 2 Townspeople Haggling with Merchant

30: 1d6 Townspeople out Shopping

31: 2d4 Townspeople Gossiping

32: 2d4 Townspeople out for a Stroll

33: 1 Pullcart with Driver and 2 Passengers

34: 1 Pullcart with Driver and No Passengers

35: 1 Pullcart with Driver and 1 Passenger

36: 1 Old War Veteran

37: 1 Wounded War Veteran Begging

38: 1 Old Man Eating

39: 2 Old Men Playing Cards

40: 1d4+1 Old Codgers Talking

41: 2d6 Old Coots

42: 2 Laborers in a Discussion

43: 1d4 Laborers Patching up the Cobblestone Street

44: 1d4+1 Laborers on Break

45: 1d6 Sailors on Leave

46: 1d6 Laborers Cleaning a Wall

47: 2d8 Laborers Constructing a Building

48: 2d8 Laborers Headed to Work

49: 2d8 Laborers on Break

50: 1 Dung Sweeper

51: 1d4 Street Sweepers

52: 1d4 Lamplighters

53: 2 Young Lovers on a Walk

54: 2 Young Lovers on a First Date

55: 2 Middle-Aged Lovers Walking Home

56: 2 Lovers Engaged in a Heated Argument

57: 2 Young Lovers Making a Nighttime Rendezvous

58: 1 Old Drunk, Barely Standing

59: 1 Old Drunk, Loudly Arguing with No One

60: 1 Old Drunk Propped Against a Wall

61: 1 Drunken Foreigner

62: 1 Lost Foreigner

63: 1d4 Workers Replacing a Destroyed Wall or Window

64: 1d6 Workers Refinishing the Surface of a Building

65: Group of 1d4+1 Tough-Looking Townsfolk, Betting on a Dogfight

66: Group of 1d4+1 Youths Gambling with Dice

67: 2d4 Drunken Rowdy Youths

68: 2 Servants Engaged in Gossip

69: 1d6 Servants Running an Errand

70: 2d4 Servants Engaged in Gossip

71: 1d4 Nervous Tourists

72: 1d4 Obvious Tourists

73: 1d4 Quiet Tourists

74: 2d4 Obvious Tourists

75: 1d6 Tourists with 1 Guide

76: 1 Street Vendor

77: 1 Artist Sketching

78: 1 Carriage with 1d4 Occupants

79: 1d4 Artists Working on a Wall Mural

80: 1 Artist Doing Street Portraits

81: 2 Men Trading a Small Item

82: 1 Old Man with Book Under His Arm

83: 1d8 Mourners Visiting a Tomb

84: 1d4 Gardeners Trimming the Topiary

85: 1 Professor with Class of 2d4 Students

86: 1 Scholar Studying His Books

87: 1d4 Stonemasons Polishing Buildings and Statuary

88: 1d4 Gardeners Replanting Uprooted Flowers

89: 1 Townsperson Buying Something from a Thief

90: 2 Craftspeople Arguing for a Noble's Business

91: 2d4 Craftspeople Arguing

92: 1d4+1 Craftspeople Arguing over a Piece of Work

93: 1 Grocer Overseeing 1d4 Porters Unloading Wagon

94: 1 Moneychanger with 2d4 Guards

95: 1 Moneychanger with 1d4 Guards

96: 1 Minor Town Official (Scribe)

97: 1 Minor Town Official (Clerk)

98: 1 Minor Official, Late for a Meeting

99: 1d4 Courtesans en route Home

100: 1d4 Courtesans with Escort of 1d4

Animals & Livestock (d8)

1: 1d6 Horses Tied Up in Front of Building

2: 2d6 Horses Tied Up in Front of Building

3: Mangy Stray Dog

4: Mangy Stray Cat

5: Pack of 2d4 Stray Dogs

6: 1d6 Livestock (Horse, oxen, sheep)

7: 1 Caravan of 2d8 Livestock (Horse, oxen, sheep)

8: Flying Object/Creature (Pegasus, magic carpet, etc.)

Traffic & Hazards (d20)

1: Slow Wagons

2: Gridlocked Wagons

3: Broken Empty Cart

4: Broken Wagon Full of Supplies

5: Stationary Empty Wagon

6: Stationary Empty Wagon with Oxen

7: Stationary Garbage Wagon Full of Street Sweepings

8: Stationary Wagon Full of Awkward Furniture

9: Stationary Wagon Being Loaded

10: 2-Wagon Collision with 1d4 Arguing Merchants and Drivers

11: 2-Carriage Collision with 1d4 Arguing Nobles and Drivers

12: Building under Construction (No Laborers Currently Present)

13: Pile of Broken Branches and Uprooted Plants, to Be Removed

14: Large Pile of Garbage, Yet to Be Hauled Away

15: Drunken Townsperson Passed Out in the Road

16: Drunken Sleeping Adventurer beside the Road

17: Old Drunk Sot Sleeping Next to a Building

18: Young Drunk Sleeping Next to a Building

19: 1 Minor Official Taking a Nap

20: Procession (see page 80)

Guards & Heroes (d20)

1: City Watch Guard

2: 2 City Watch Guards

3: City Watch Patrol (2d4)

4: City Watch Squad (2d6)

5: Town Guard Detachment (4d6)

6: Veteran Fighter

7: Veteran Mercenary

8: Foreign Mercenary

9: Drunk Mercenary

10: 1d4 Drunk Mercenaries

11: 1d4+1 Mercenaries Arguing

12: 1d4+1 Mercenaries Looking for a Fight

13: Actual Magician (Not disguised)

14: Actual Magician (Disguised)

15: Private Warehouse Guard

16: 1 Adventurer

17: 1 Drunk Adventurer

18: 1d3 Drunk Adventurers

19: 1d3 Adventurers Looking for a Fight

20: Adventuring Party (1d4+1 Adventurers)

Priests & Preachers (d12)

1: 1 Ragged Priest(ess) Talking to Themself

2: 1 Ragged Evangelist

3: 1 Priest(ess)

4: 1 Priest(ess) with 1d8 Followers

5: 1 Priest(ess) with Class of 4d6 Students

6: 1 Preacher with Quiet Crowd of 3d12

7: 1 Preacher Riling Up a Crowd of 4d12

8: 2 Priest(ess)es in a Religious Discussion

9: 1d6 Beggar Monks Begging for Alms

10: 1d4+1 Priests/Priestesses

11: 2d6 Priests Exhorting to the Masses

12: Major Religious Figure

Performers & Entertainers (d10)

1: Street Magician

2: Street Juggler

3: Street Performer/Actor

4: Street Minstrel

5: Strolling Minstrel

6: 1d4 Gladiators Demonstrating Combat

7: Dancing Bear with Owner

8: Performing Animal with Owner

9: Juggler Being Harassed by His Audience

10: Torchlight Celebration

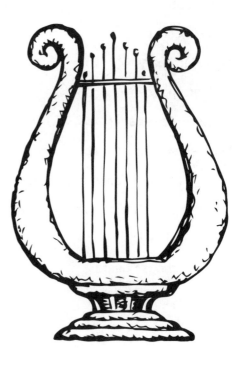

Merchants & Businessfolk (d20)

1: 1 Local Merchant

2: 1 Merchant in Front of Their Store

3: 1 Merchant Headed Home

4: 1 Merchant Making a Delivery on Foot

5: 1 Merchant Making a Delivery in Wagon

6: 1 Foreign Merchant

7: 1 Lost Foreign Merchant

8: 1 Exotic or Non-Human Merchant

9: 1 Merchant Making a Sale to 1 Customer

10: 1 Merchant Making a Sale to 1d2 Customers

11: 1 Merchant Making a Sale to 1d4 Customers

12: 1 Merchant Haggling with 1d8 Customers

13: 1 Merchant Flattering a Noble

14: 1 Merchant Haggling with 2 Adventurers

15: 2 Merchants in a Heated Debate

16: 2 Merchants Haggling

17: 2 Foreign Merchants Arguing in Different Languages

18: 2 Foreign Caravan Owners Arguing in Different Languages

19: 1d4 Merchants Chatting Outside of Their Closed Shop

20: 1d4 Merchants Delivering to a Noble

Messengers & Speakers (d20)

1: Wild-Eyed Speaker on a Crate

2: Unremarkable Messenger

3: Messenger Scanning the Crowd for Some Particular Person

4: Messenger in Guild Livery

5: Messenger for a Merchant Consortium

6: Messenger in Local Government's Regalia

7: Messenger in Noble House Regalia

8: Runner Delivering a Small Item (Jewelry, weapon, etc.)

9: Crier with Printed One-Sheet Pamphlets

11: Crier for Local Food Vendor

12: Crier for Local Restaurant

13: Crier Advertising Merchant's Goods

14: Crier Announcing the Arrival of a Shipment

15: Crier Advertising Theater/Entertainment

16: Crier Advertising Local Event/Celebration

17: Crier Announcing an Upcoming Holiday/Festival

18: Crier Loudly Announcing City News

19: Crier in Noble Regalia

20: Political Crier and 2d12 Listeners

Nobles & Royals (d20)

1: 1 Noble in a Simple Litter with 1 Bearer

2: 1 Noble in a Fancy Palanquin with 2 Bearers

3: 1 Noble Out for a Walk

4: 1 Noble Directing Construction

5: 1 Young Noble Out for a Walk

6: 1 Young Noble Being Loud and Rude

7: 1 Noble Drunk and Stumbling

8: 1 Noble Returning from Shopping with 1d4 Bearers

9: 1 Noble Out for a Walk with 1d4 Bodyguards

10: 1 Young Noble, Drunk and Stumbling

11: 2 Nobles in a Discussion

12: 2 Nobles in an Argument

13: 1d4 Nobles Out for a Walk

14: 1d4 Nobles Looking for a Fight

15: 1d4 Young Nobles Out for a Walk

16: 1d4 Young Nobles, Drunk and Stumbling

17: 1d4 Young Nobles Looking for a Fight

18: Group of 1d4 Nobles and 2d6 Retainers

19: 1d4 Nobles in a Carriage with Noble Livery

20: Royal Retinue (1d6+1 Nobles and 3d6 Retainers)

Tavern Patrons (d20)

Among adventurers, an impromptu bar crawl or visit to the local watering hole for information could happen at any moment. Roll here if you need to whip up some random patrons at your local establishment. Each is guaranteed to have at least 1d4 rumors, clues, or hints to push characters in the right direction.

Patron	Description
1: Musician	Sings and plays a variety of instruments. Picks up information from listening to other tavern patrons while he plays.
2: Storyteller	Recites epic poems and well-known local tales. Learns ancient and lost lore from their stories, as well as juicy rumors and gossip.
3: Performer	Juggles, dances, or has an animal companion who does tricks while the performer bangs a tambourine. Knows high-society gossip.
4: Waiter/Barmaid	Runs around the tavern serving drinks and taking orders. Picks up information overheard from various other tables.
5: Bartender	Takes money, delivers drinks, and guards the till. Picks up rumors from drunk clientele who say more than they should at late hours.
6: Innkeeper	Oversees the staff and guards, looks out for troublemakers. Learns information based on who has stayed at which taverns and inns in town.
7: Adventurer	Hangs out, drinks, boasts, and performs semi-impressive tricks to win over the crowd. Has picked up information from former party members and adventuring companions.
8: Traveler	Looks lonesome and quiet at the bar, goes to bed early to set out before first light. Has learned information from nearby towns that they have traveled through.
9: Merchant	Nervously avoids unsavory-looking individuals, but loudly offers wares and displays of wealth to any potential buyers. Learns information from their business contacts and customers.
10: Local Hero	Keeps an eye on things, helps those in need, defends the town. Picks up rumors from those they have saved, usually in the form of requests for help.
11: Local Shopkeeper	Relaxes during downtime, enjoys the local company, listens to nearby industry-related conversations. Knows information about the economics and industrial aspects of town.

Patron	Description
12: Local Worker	Relaxes during downtime, enjoys the local company, and may get involved in revelry or trouble depending on how late the hour. Knows rumors that have spread around the working-class folk.
13: Troublemaker	Instigates trouble with the characters, or provokes someone else to do so. Knows rumors being spread around the more unsavory circles of town.
14: Supernatural Being	Stays quiet and reserved, but displays some almost-hidden sign of their true nature. Alternatively, they are not hiding their true nature at all, yet all tavern patrons are comfortable with this presence for some reason. Knows information and lore from the spiritual and magical world.
15: Off-Duty Guardsman	Relaxes during downtime, but stays alert to danger and comes down hard on any criminal activity. Learns rumors by interrogating criminals and other villainous characters.
16: Undercover Spy	Watches on behalf of a mysterious faction or individual, may be spying on the characters. Has a great deal of information, but little incentive to share any of it.
17: Youth	Is just excited to be here, drinks, and idolizes/imitates the characters if given the opportunity. Knows good information that people have said in front of them, thinking them too naive to understand.
18: Couple	Flirt and fawn over each other, maybe a little too aggressively. They know information from around town; because they are two, they have twice as much info, but take four times as long to convey it due to… distractions.
19: Old Man	Talks to himself, spins yarns, and reminisces about the old days. Knows old information that only an old local would know.
20: Mysterious Stranger	Lurks in the corner booth and watches. Knows some terrible secret, either about the town, the future, or about one of the characters in particular. (Refer to page 78.)

Unique Tavern Features (d20)

Every tavern has a unique feature, but the best ones have something truly memorable to keep locals and adventurers alike coming back for more. Roll here to see what kind of special detail sets a particular establishment apart.

Feature	Description
1: Haunted	Is possessed by the spirit of a former owner, patron, adventurer, or other person with close connections to the building. The ghost might be innocuous, a minor pest, or a rare but violent threat.
2: Mysterious Sounds	Plagued by a mysterious or supernatural source of music or other sounds (rats, thumping, etc.). No one can seem to pinpoint the source of the sound; maybe they have stopped trying.
3: Competitive Crowd	Hosts a number of different official or unofficial contests that visitors are always encouraged to participate in. The contests are probably friendly, but that doesn't mean they can't get quite violent.
4: Armed and Armored	Frequented by patrons who always carry weapons and wear full armor while relaxing and drinking here, either as a safety precaution or as an aesthetic choice.
5: Comfortable Furnishings	Furnished with especially nice beds, seating, and other amenities to provide travelers with restful relaxation. They may even come equipped with bathing or massage services.
6: Fine Food	Has a reputation for exceptionally high-quality food. When rolling the food menu (page 158) for this establishment, add an extra + (1d4 x 10) to your rolls.
7: Fine Drinks	Has a reputation for exceptionally high-quality drinks. When rolling the drink menu (page 162) for this establishment, add an extra + (1d4 x 10) to your rolls.
8: No Weapons Allowed	Forbids weapons of any kind and has a bouncer who frisks visitors at the door. They may be savvy enough to recognize magical weapons or tricks.
9: Neighborhood Dive	Caters far more to locals than it does to travelers. Whether a high- or low-class establishment, the regulars might not take kindly to outsiders coming into their watering hole.
10: Guarded	Local stop for the town guard once their duties are complete. Off-duty guards are still guards, however, and troublemakers might not realize the danger until it is already too late.

Feature	Description
11: Odd Smell	Perfectly ordinary, but a lingering odor—either delicious, disgusting, or strange—continually persists, despite all attempts to expunge it.
12: House of Comfort	Caters to clientele looking to relax through more than just sleeping (though it may not be obvious to the untrained eye). Patrons of all kinds are welcome, and this tavern is probably a sight classier than a typical brothel.
13: Entertaining	Spares no expense when it comes to providing its patrons with stellar entertainment. Has more than its share of bards and other performers, with potentially multiple entertainers performing at the same time, including non-musical acts and other shows.
14: Unique Patronage	Caters to a specific subset of the town's population. This unique group may be a specific faction, occupation, or race. The nature of the group will determine how welcome outsiders are.
15: Blessed	Blessed by a local deity or church in some official or visually obvious way and may cater exclusively to members of that particular religion.
16: Hall of Trophies	Has a particularly large collection of hunting trophies. Roll 2d6 times (or more) on the Stuffed Heads table (see page 166) to see what manner of trophies are present.
17: Perpetually Endangered	Built on the edge of some border—mystical or otherwise—which results in monsters and/or enemies occasionally slipping through to attack patrons. The tavern is at least somewhat prepared to deal with these incursions.
18: College Bar	Caters particularly to the local students who attend a nearby university or other learning institution, such as a school for craftsfolk or magicians.
19: Famous Owner	The owner is a figure of repute within the community: a retired hero, the king or mayor, or a well-connected crime boss. Adventurers who make problems here will pay the price later.
20: Legendary	Known throughout the land, either due to popular opinion or historical fame. The characters might not know the exact reason for this reputation, a fact which locals will take personally.

Mysterious Strangers (d20)

The figure in the back of the tavern: there is always one (and if there's not, the characters will find one). Roll here to see what this particular mysterious stranger is up to.

Stranger	Description
1: Magical	The magical nature of this mysterious stranger is obvious. Their wings, horns, glowing eyes, tail, sparkling skin, or other feature marks them unmistakably as supernatural.
2: Wizened	Incredible age has made this mysterious stranger knowledgeable. They may be even older than they look and recollect impossible information from eons past.
3: Forbidden	A dark reputation surrounds this mysterious stranger. Whether it was earned or merely the result of an unsettling appearance or aura, the whole tavern fears interacting with this individual.
4: Silent	Due to physical inability or choice, this mysterious stranger does not speak under any circumstances. Even when approached, they either fail to respond or communicate through other means.
5: Illusion	This mysterious stranger is not all they appear to be. Indeed, interaction may reveal that physical objects pass right through the stranger. No one knows why the illusionary duplicate was sent, or whom they are a copy of.
6: Wanted	Wanted posters for this mysterious stranger may be hanging in this tavern or nearby establishments. They have a bounty on their head and are on the run from the law.
7: For Hire	While they are not advertising their services, this mysterious stranger is amenable to helping adventurers in need—for a price. They will accept if asked by anyone with enough money or skill to impress them.
8: Peanut Gallery	This mysterious stranger will quickly identify themselves as the unofficial comedian of the bar. They continually quip and poke fun at anyone unfortunate enough to garner their attention, heedless of the danger to their well-being.
9: Challenger	Any trouble in this establishment is quickly met by this imposing figure. On behalf of the patrons, they settle any quarrels that visiting adventurers might raise.
10: Mystical	The magical prowess of this mysterious stranger is not immediately obvious, but woe be upon anyone foolish enough to cross them. They likely possess abilities far beyond that of their challengers.

Stranger	Description
11: Questgiver	While they may avoid approaching adventurers in obvious ways, this mysterious stranger is desperately seeking to make contact with heroes who can help them. They carry on their person a scroll, map, or journal which points the way to an item that they need.
12: Old Friend	This figure only seems to be a stranger; in reality, they know one of the characters in the party from their maybe-distant past. They may be in town to spy upon their old compatriot, track them down, or pursue their own unrelated goals.
13: Criminal	Within the tavern, it is a known secret that this mysterious stranger has regular dealings with the town's criminal underworld. They do not seem to fear arrest, being a "made" criminal with powerful connections.
14: Woodsman	This gruff mysterious stranger seems like they could be a villain, but in reality is a noble woodland ranger from the wilds near town. They may be in town on a mission or as part of their standard watch duties.
15: Mourner	It is obvious that this mysterious stranger is distressed, but it is not clear what their problem is. In fact, this stranger has lost a loved one to some tragedy or danger—something adventurers might be able to rectify.
16: Stalker	Unbeknownst to the characters, they have acquired a fan whose devotion borderlines on obsession. This mysterious stranger is devoted, perhaps even in love with, one or more of the characters.
17: Rival	This mysterious stranger keeps a careful eye on one of the characters. Whether or not they have ever actually met before, this stranger has a vendetta to settle against this character for a past grievance (perceived or otherwise).
18: Lost Child	Whether they are eerily silent or bawling for their mother, the real mystery is how this child came to be in the tavern in the first place. They can just barely communicate the nature of the danger that separated them from their parents.
19: Low-Key Merchant	Though they do not advertise their wares, this mysterious stranger deals in illegal, dangerous, or forbidden goods. They may only have a single, rare item to sell, but the exchange must be secret, and it must be final.
20: Future Self	This mysterious stranger is one of the characters from the future and has returned to spy upon their past self. They have no desire to interact with their past self and change the time stream, so they will use all of their power to avoid this.

Street Parades (d20)

Nothing brings traffic (and heart-pounding chase scenes) to an abrupt halt quite like a street parade! Large groups of moving townsfolk might be just the thing to either get in the characters' way, or provide the cover they need to escape. Roll here to determine the nature of a certain migration making its way through your town.

Parade Type	Description
1: Student Procession	The students of a local school or university parade down the street to or from school as a celebration of the beginning or end of the school year. The students might be freshman recruits or the graduating class.
2: Riot	The people of the town are enraged over some injustice, perceived or real, and have begun to get violent and destructive. Even characters who try to stay clear are at risk of getting caught in the crossfire.
3: Trade Show	A particular guild or industry has organized a parade wherein crafters may show off their finest and most valuable wares by proudly carting or carrying them up and down the streets for customers to see.
4: Livestock Show	Farmers and handlers are parading cows, horses, sheep, or some other celebrated local livestock around town. Even more than human traffic, this may provide an obstacle to anyone trying to get anywhere in a hurry.
5: Military Display	The local lord or lady has ordered their troops to march in the streets as a show of pride, strength, and authority. The people may love or despise this powerful display.
6: Protest	The people of the town are parading through the streets, expressing their displeasure with a new law or edict. They may press the issue with the characters, trying to learn their thoughts and loyalties regarding local politics.
7: Independence	The parade is celebrating the independence of the town or kingdom from some enemy or oppressor. National loyalties are at an all-time high, and characters from the rival nation or faction may be in danger.
8: Floats	This parade is a celebration traditionally marked by huge floats, balloons, or simply wagons stacked high with fantastic artistic displays. These floats can prove difficult to navigate around, especially during a fight.
9: Musical	This parade is filled with celebratory music and dancing in the streets. Characters who join in performing must be sure to know the traditional tunes or hymns or risk gravely insulting the celebrants.

Parade Type	Description
10: Feast Day	This parade celebrates the life of a blessed saint or holy person. Images of the saint are represented in statue, painting, and even costume form everywhere in town.
11: Holy Day	This parade celebrates a grave and serious holy day and has a somber feel to it. The event might rile up fanatics and others with less tolerance toward other religions and faiths.
12: Fool's Day	This parade is a celebration of laughter, pranks, and chaos. The participants may engage in fun-loving revelry with the characters, or might instead try to make them victims of the topsy-turvy nature of the festival.
13: Hero's Feast	This parade celebrates the life and deeds, or perhaps one particular deed, of a single hero of legend. The hero may be a local legend whom the characters have revealed additional information about.
14: Day of Death	Skeletons, ghosts, and other decorations fill this parade with a macabre aesthetic. The celebrants are wild and joyous, as though to embrace life and the living even as they celebrate its end.
15: Sacrificial	This procession is slowly marching out of town to a nearby hilltop, river, tree, or mound in order to perform a traditional ritual sacrifice upon it. The nature of the sacrifice could be simple (grain, apples) or terrifying (children, enemy soldiers).
16: Pride Day	This parade celebrates a traditionally underrepresented or oppressed minority within the town. Some may take issue with the position of the celebrants, but the food and clothes are objectively fantastic.
17: Funeral	This solemn, silent procession carries candles and a casket as they march to the graveyard to lay one of their own to rest. This death may portend future woes, or highlight current ones, for the community.
18: Mock Funeral	This solemn, silent procession carries candles and a casket as though for a funeral. In reality, the casket is empty. Locals know this tradition is symbolic of a historical death of great importance, but strangers might be surprised.
19: Fertility Festival	This parade celebrates the spring bloom, new life, and healthy children—not to mention all that goes with it. The festival is generally positive, but some of its old-fashioned traditions and costumes make some spectators in the crowd visibly uncomfortable.
20: Impromptu Crowd	This mob of townsfolk isn't crowding the streets for a parade but has gathered here unexpectedly to witness something. Perhaps a crime, accident, street performance, or some other more serious incident has drawn a great deal of attention.

Bard Songs (d20)

Brave heroes require rest and relaxation in between their adventures; and no night at a tavern is complete without entertainment. Roll here if the characters are wondering what's playing in the common room (or maybe through the unfortunately thin floorboards of their room). Whether the goal is revelry, theft, or seduction, the right soundtrack can make all the difference!

Bard Song	Description
1: Song of Rupert	Recounts the exploits of one Rupert, a local hero of legend who seems to have attained an unimaginable level of status and respect, the likes of which the characters could never achieve. Tavern patrons will, quietly or loudly, size up characters in comparison to the descriptions of Rupert—reputedly strong, tall, and handsome to the extreme, and a victor at more than a few barroom wrestling matches and brawls.
2: Me Olde Faire Lady	A song sure to get the entire tavern clapping, stomping, and dancing along. Traditionally two dancers, a man and a woman, link hands in the center of the tavern on a table and perform an elaborate somersaulting dance without breaking grip. Falling off the table disqualifies the dancers but entertains the crowd thoroughly. The pinnacle of peasant entertainment.
3: The Dust and Darkness	A slow and sober tune that recounts the exploits of a group of adventurers who explored a nearby dungeon and never returned. In each verse, a hero is killed off, until the final hero dies of loneliness. The bard who has to follow this act is very annoyed, as the song is a notorious room-killer and often upsets passing adventurers.
4: Fiddly-doo	This extremely catchy tavern tune is easy to learn, popular among children, and once stuck in your head, never leaves. Some people in town absolutely love Fiddly-doo, and some people despise it; the division between these two camps can grow quite heated, to the point where even so much as humming the tune in front of the wrong person can result in a fight breaking out.
5: Dunder the Dragon	A song about a hero who goes off to slay a particularly foolish and gullible dragon. The song mocks every new misunderstanding and trick played upon the dragon, who ends up slowly losing its entire hoard to the hero. The story may be about a real dragon who lives in the local area, but it may not be an entirely accurate account of the events.

Bard Song	Description
6: Moonlight & Fire	A romantic song about two lovers who must see each other from afar, across a lake, where they both light fires on opposite shores so as to better see each other's silhouettes. The fire helps them to know where to look for each other, but when the fires go out, the moon illuminates the lake and allows them to see each other clearly. A happy ending, unless you know the whole story, which is not part of the song.
7: Wine on the Riverboat	A joyous, celebratory song typically associated with riverboat sailors and revelry. The chorus is a well-known bit about "not tipping over the boat," imitating a drunken crew running to and fro and tipping the deck of a boat back and forth. The lyrics are known throughout the land, even in landlocked cities and towns, making this a wonderful song for getting folks into a friendly drinking mood.
8: Old Charlie's Last Stand	A somber but familiar tune about a friend (always dearly beloved to the narrator) named Charlie who took on every challenge and met even the most casual dare. The long list of Old Charlie's exploits culminates in him dying while accomplishing some now-famous feat, which he is praised for completing while simultaneously being so foolish, heroic, and drunk.
9: Red Blades & Red Banners	A political song that is liable to cause problems, or at least heightened tensions, wherever it is played. It recounts a well-known battle (some say a rebellion or a riot) in recent history, the political fallout of which still causes a lot of pain and suffering in the region today. Singers should expect either anger or silence in reaction to this song; both reactions are bad.
10: The Night-Witch's Song	A haunting melody accompanies this song about the ghost of a local woman, a shrieking, eyeless entity that still roams the forests. The stories about this woman's hexes upon men who slighted her love are almost certainly false; the true fate she suffered in life is certainly being kept a secret by someone in town. The song may give clues as to the identity of her true abuser or murderer.
11: The Traveling Man	A singalong tune in which the narrator recounts the journeys of the eponymous Traveling Man, who visits many of the familiar countries and famously scenic locations in the world. Some of these locations may be places the characters have visited previously, or will foreshadow their visits in the future. Others might be places they will never go to, but which are nonetheless important to their story.

Bard Song	Description
12: The Night of Burning Trees	This epic war ballad tells the story of a famous battle that occurred nearby, possibly on the town's current location (possibly this battle was even involved in the foundation of the town). The battle was a particularly cinematic one, with the image of trees burning against a night sky illuminating soldiers locked in mortal combat as the central motif.
13: Dance of the Daggers	This song from another, distant land tells the story of an evil emperor who was slain by a beautiful assassin. The assassin tricked him into thinking that she was a dancer/concubine and let his guard down at just the right moment. The song might have been altered from its original narrative to adapt to the local culture in ways that only certain characters might notice.
14: The Winds over White Waves	A haunting, slow song about the natural beauty of a particular nearby beach or waterfront. Important features (rocks, lighthouses, shipwrecks) are highlighted, as well as local legends about ghosts and pirates in the area. A potential clue to a treasure or quest location in the area might easily be slipped into the lyrics.
15: The Man from Out of Town	This song tells the story of a mysterious stranger who appeared at various times and places to help various people throughout the town's history. It is clear that the man is some manner of supernatural entity or magician, but it is never explicitly made known who or what the "Man" is, only that his intentions seem to be, at least as far as the town can tell, sincerely benevolent.
16: South of the Hills	A fun-loving song about the various creatures, people, and places that can be found south (or a direction of your choice) of town. The song makes the land south of town sound like a curious and confusing place; in reality, it is full of misunderstandings and misinformation about the denizens and locations. The song is heavily dated, to say the least.
17: Good King Cleaver	"King Cleaver" was a local politician who may or may not have been a real king; suffice to say, "Cleaver" was a fake, albeit well-earned nickname for his reign of terror. The song includes numerous unflattering descriptions of his physical appearance, hygiene, and mannerisms, as well as attributing to him personally an unlikely amount of human butchery and cannibalism.

Bard Song	Description
18: Song of Rest	This hymn to a gentle, benevolent deity asks for the various different blessings which she grants, which include simple pleasures such as a hot bath, a good night's sleep, good food, and good friendship. The song claims that the deity takes pity upon travelers in particular and may bless those who honor the singer of the hymn.
19: Summer Luck	A drinking song about gambling with dice, the lyrics speak of a gambler on a lucky streak that only ends at the end of the song (at which point the final fate of the gambler varies depending on the singer). The metaphor of summer and winter as representing the inevitability of good and bad luck streaks recurs throughout the song.
20: Bewitching Song	This song seems to have no words, but the melody is enchanting; literally, it seems to have some bewitching effect upon the crowd, such as making them happy or sad, lulling them to sleep or intoxication, or simply making them eager to sing and clap along. The singer may be aware of the power they wield, or just as clueless as the audience members listening.

Bard Quirks (d20)

The bard is the centerpiece of any tavern, and the quality of their performance will set the tone of the whole evening. Roll here to see what kind of bard the local establishment has hired for the night.

Bard Quirk	Description
1: Off-Key	Not every musician can be perfect, but this one is particularly bad at their craft. It is a wonder that they ever stumbled into this career, and unlikely that they do not recognize their own lack of skill. For a non-singer, substitute any kind of analogous incompetence that you see fit.
2: Overconfident	This bard is perfectly adequate, but does not nearly possess the grandmaster-level of skill and training they believe themselves to have. They may attempt to aggressively one-up anyone they perceive as a potential rival. Any truly experienced adventurer will recognize the nature of this impostor almost immediately.
3: Lack of Confidence	This bard has decent abilities and a lot of potential, but absolutely zero faith in their performance. They consistently ask for the crowd's approval and apologize constantly for any perceived lack of satisfaction on the part of the audience. A little encouragement, a small confidence boost, would go a long way with this one.
4: Surprisingly Young	This bard couldn't be older than fourteen summers, and yet can play and sing and dance as well as the best and most experienced performers. No explanation is given for their unusual abilities, for the youth has learned to trust no one with their secrets, whether they be mundane (they received expert training as a child) or magical (they are not really a youth at all).
5: Old and Weathered	This bard is an aged and decrepit specimen of their trade, although their elderly state may or may not impact their performing abilities. They are certainly experienced, knowing songs and lore long forgotten by other locals and travelers alike. Not only that, but their own personal insights may shed light upon times and events previously only understood secondhand by the characters.
6: Lyrically Inaccurate	This bard's music is fine, but they can't seem to get any of the words right. They either change the lyrics on the spot (much to the frustration of those who know the proper words and actually care about such things) or forget them entirely, fumbling and guessing with little regard for accuracy.

Bard Quirk	Description
7: Professional Propagandist	This bard is a plant sent by some political faction to intentionally mislead or twist the public perception toward their favor (or against an opponent). They tell stories and sing songs that have been deliberately altered to skew the historical record in an advantageous way.
8: Deliberately Misleading	This bard, for personal reasons, has taken up a campaign of misinformation. They enact topical performances, with the intention of either encouraging or defaming the reputation of some well-known figure. Their motives most likely involve jealous vengeance of some kind, perhaps over a dramatic love triangle.
9: Overenthusiastic	This bard is just a bit too lively for the crowd. It might seem nice at first, but quickly begins to grate on the audience. Any attempts to engage the bard only encourage and exacerbate the situation, as the characters get dragged further into the "fun."
10: Bored	This bard clearly has better places to be than playing here at this tavern tonight; or, at least, they wish they did. They barely put any effort into their duties, and don't seem to notice whether or not the crowd is enjoying itself. If no one stops them, this bard will attempt to pack up and leave early, plunging the common room into awkward, uncomfortable silence.
11: Ill, Sick, Hoarse	This bard has seen better days. Whether due to a sudden onset of sickness, or some prolonged malady, they are stuck with a physical hindrance (shaky hands, croaking voice, etc.), which is impacting their ability to perform. The show must go on, but no one is enjoying themselves.
12: Physical Danger	This bard is doing just fine entertaining the audience, but not for the reasons they think. Certain elements of their performance (knives, fire, general clumsiness) present a physical danger to the patrons around them. The characters must be wary to avoid becoming unintentional casualties of the show.
13: Impossibly Beautiful	This bard is impossibly, perhaps even supernaturally, gifted when it comes to their physical appearance. This may be due to a mysterious ancestry or magical boon, or simple good luck on the bard's part. Seductive characters beware; this bard has heard it all before.
14: Sincere Friend	This bard has reason to be trusted. They may have singled out one character as a fellow compatriot due to some shared background, or have a special motivation for showing empathy to the characters in general, but their motives for wanting to help are generally sincere.

Bard Quirk	Description
15: Scholar	This bard is extremely well-read about some field of expertise, such as ancient history or local area knowledge. They might be a valuable resource to characters looking for insight, but the price they'll pay for such information may not be coin, but rather other information and rumors—tit for tat.
16: Impossibly Gifted	This bard's talents are not merely impressive—they are incredibly, impossibly, suspiciously good. There may be nefarious origins to these talents, but the bard is unlikely to have any ulterior motive beyond winning fame and fortune through the application of their skills. There may still be a price of some manner to be paid, however.
17: Cloying Flatter	This bard is always looking for well-known heroes and other local celebrities to latch onto as a way to advance their own career. They will attempt to flatter and flirt their way into a friendly relationship with the characters in order to pump them for stories and other social clout. This panderer is an expert manipulator, however, and may not take no for an answer.
18: Impoverished	This bard is in a desperate financial situation and may very well end up out on the streets if this night's performance does not go well. Their desperation puts a nervous edge on their performance, and their constant pleas for donations may grow distracting.
19: Fan	This bard is just a little too excited to meet heroic adventurers like the characters. They are eager to latch onto any upcoming expeditions as a hanger-on and documentarian of the characters' exploits. The dangers of having such a rube around are readily apparent.
20: Mysterious Stranger	Little is known about this bard, save that they always arrive in town without ever being seen, and depart just as quickly and quietly as they first appeared. Their origins may indeed be supernatural, or they may just value the sense of mystery and drama for performance purposes.

Healer Quirks (d20)

Characters often return to town when they need healing. Not everyone has the time or patience to wait for nature to take its course, and sometimes magical or mundane healers are needed. Every healer is different, however, and sometimes exchanging coin for health is not so simple.

Healer Quirk	Description
1: Fanatic	This healer is a religious zealot. They may refuse the character service if they do not share the same faith, or attempt conversion throughout their stay—either subtly or not-so-subtly.
2: Experimental	This healer wants to learn more about the body by experimenting on patients, and may blur or outright cross the line of consent with their testing. Whatever "upgrades" they offer may work, but always at a price.
3: Natural	This healer is focused on the natural world as a source of their healing arts. They will take any recent offenses committed against the local wildlife or land as personal insults and refuse services to such despoilers.
4: Supplier	This healer supplies the community with a potion, herb, or drug upon which they have become dependent or addicted. They may view their dealings as a mercy, or a necessary evil, but the substance is causing long-term problems.
5: Probation	This healer has been forbidden from performing certain advanced portions of their craft due to legal concerns, lack of proper qualifications, or simple bureaucracy. The characters will only get partial service until a bribe makes it worth the healer's while.
6: Educated	This healer's knowledge and wisdom goes above and beyond even that high standard typically displayed within the craft. Due to old age, or experience acquired through other hardships, they are unparalleled within their field.
7: Military	Whether or not they are currently on duty, this healer has close connections to the military of the region. Their loyalty to the local soldiers may cause them to be especially alert to foreign spies and enemies of the land.
8: Municipal	This healer offers their services under the official blessing of the town. They may serve as a special healer for the town guard; criminals will not be welcome here. And while they may be funded by the town, this does not necessarily mean that services are free.

Healer Quirk	Description
9: Engineer	This healer's experience with restoring health to the body is only one facet of their interest in the physical world. They have other interests, such as the mixing of chemical compounds or the construction of mechanical devices, of which the characters may make use.
10: Blank	This healer's expression is puzzlingly hard to read. This makes predicting their diagnoses for complicated health matters extremely frustrating. It may cause patients to assume that they are inept at their work, which could be the case entirely.
11: Scarred	Some accident has left this healer scarred, burnt, or otherwise burdened with long-term injuries. It may have been a result of their work or an incident that happened prior to their interest in healing.
12: Personal Physician	This healer has connections to someone of influence, perhaps even one of the leaders of the land. These connections could be exploited by the characters to nefarious ends. Or, if one of the characters is themselves a proficient healer, other lucrative opportunities may arise.
13: Community-Focused	This healer cares above all for the local population of their town or neighborhood. Their nearly parental attachment may make them overprotective, to the point where they overstep their authority and try to control the lives of the community in unwanted ways.
14: Incompetent	It's not a question of whether or not this healer is bad at their job. It's a question of how good they are at hiding it. And how long it takes the characters to notice it. They may be a well-meaning buffoon or a genuine charlatan, but either way, they are liable to do more harm than good if allowed near a patient.
15: Disillusioned	This healer, due to some long-term or sudden trauma, has become despondent and unwilling to do more than the most basic healing. They will need to be inspired into believing that saving lives can make a difference at all if they are to put their talents to work.
16: Inexperienced	Though perfectly talented, this healer simply hasn't had much experience. Due to youth, isolation, or relative safety, they haven't had much opportunity to put their healing craft to the test. If the characters show any lack of faith, it only makes the healer more nervous.
17: Religious	This healer is deeply religious, even holding a rank within their church hierarchy. However, they don't display the signs of their faith or speak of it unless they are directly asked by, or on intimate terms with, a character.

Healer Quirk	Description
18: Patronizing	This healer belittles every wound, making the characters out to be infants for needing medical attention. They heal every wound brought before them, but the characters will never hear the end of it.
19: Indentured	This healer was once a prisoner or captive from an enemy faction. Now, through desperation or natural assimilation, they have become a valued part of the community and offer their services like any local healer. Those who still begrudge them have not yet needed their healing touch.
20: Mad Scientist	This healer has an adventure that they want to take the characters on, and there's just no time to wait! There is a high likelihood that proposed supernatural mission will involve dimensional travel, time travel, entering dreams, entering living organisms, or all of the above.

Guard Captain Quirks (d20)

The town guard is a large force, but they typically answer to central leadership. Those who form the ranks might have a contentious relationship with their leadership, or the two might influence each other. Roll here to determine what kind of a leader is in charge of the guards as a whole, or of a particular squad or brigade.

Guard Quirk	Description
1: Near Retirement	This captain might be one year, one day, or literally one hour from retirement. They are getting too old for this shit.
2: Grizzled (Experienced)	This captain isn't necessarily old but has been at their job for more than a decade and has learned a thing or two. They have a realistic and pragmatic approach to their duties.
3: War Veteran	This captain served in the military, possibly during a major war. Their experiences have colored how they carry out their duties and discipline criminals and other subordinate guards.
4: Woodsperson	This captain has lived most of their life in or around the woodlands or other wilderness surrounding the city. They are experienced at navigating the wilds and protecting them from criminals and evildoers.
5: Suspicious	This captain is extremely paranoid, even toward outsiders who have done nothing against the town. They will always assume the worst when it comes to the characters' actions.
6: Friendly	This captain is a jovial and kind individual. They would rather let a criminal off with a warning or rehabilitate them than lock them up or punish them.
7: Beloved	This captain is well-loved by the citizens of the town, either for their even-handed justice or for some heroic deed they accomplished in the past. The people will always side with them, even if the captain is secretly working against the town.
8: Ordinary Citizen	This captain is accepted by most townspeople as just "one of the folks." In some ways, this makes them especially trusted by the community; conversely, the townsfolk might not actually honor the authority and special privileges of office that this captain deserves.
9: Slayer	This captain has a reputation for defeating a particular type of monster or enemy. They either defeat these foes on a regular basis or have defeated particularly impressive examples of this enemy.
10: Investigative Knack	This captain has an uncanny instinct for uncovering clues and evidence against wrongdoing. They will quickly sniff out any loose ends the characters have left on any of their criminal activities.

Guard Quirk	Description
11: By-the-Books	This captain makes certain to always follow the letter of their duties, rather than the spirit of the law. Whether due to their personality, circumstances, or strict oversight, they won't budge when it comes to enforcing even the most minor laws.
12: Loose Cannon	This captain is impulsive and headstrong, seeking justice (or at least vengeance against crime) at any cost. They will bend or break the law to accomplish their goals.
13: Paranoid	This captain is constantly in a state of anxiety over whether their town, the guards, or they themselves are in danger. Their fears may be valid, especially in a dangerous or unsavory town, but they only serve to make the captain their own worst enemy.
14: Overworked	This captain is kept incredibly busy at all hours, with barely any time for tackling new crimes and developments in town. This may be due to the sheer volume or stakes of the crimes being committed, or due to corruption, excessive paperwork, or other circumstances that keep the captain occupied.
15: Idealistic	This captain cannot be corrupted, bribed, or otherwise convinced to betray their ideals. They will gladly take a criminal down for no other reason than the principle of law and order.
16: Reluctantly Corrupt	This captain is being paid off, but has second thoughts about the arrangement due to moral compunctions, fear of reprisal, or anxiety about the long-term consequences. They can be persuaded to rethink the arrangement and possibly even betray their masters.
17: Happily Corrupt	This captain is being paid off by criminals, the wealthy, or some political faction in order to either help advance their agenda or to look the other way on some issue. They are happy with the arrangement and will work to preserve their extra income.
18: Secret Criminal	This captain is in league with, or perhaps the secret leader of, the local criminal underworld. They use their position of power to better perpetrate their crimes.
19: Magical Law-Enforcer	This captain is either a spellcaster or has powers or knowledge at their disposal to hunt down and arrest other magicians (or at least those suspected of magic).
20: Divine Protector	This captain has been chosen by the gods to protect the city. They might have a supernatural nature or powers that may or may not be hidden from the townspeople.

Weaponsmith Quirks (d20)

Characters are often on the lookout for weapons with which to defend themselves; not all care about who or where they get those weapons from. But some weapon crafters or arms dealers might react differently to foreign vagabonds rolling into town looking for tools for killing. Roll here to find out more about the friendly local weaponsmith.

Weaponsmith Quirk	Description
1: Philanthropist	This weaponsmith has a soft spot for those in need and can be persuaded by good and noble causes. Their work supports the community, and cheating them is a good way to get blacklisted by the town at large.
2: Monster Hunter	This weaponsmith knows the right weapon to use against the right monster. They know the strengths and weaknesses of supernatural and magical enemies, as well as more mundane deadly predators, and can recommend the tool for a given job.
3: Ammunition Specialist	This weaponsmith specializes in odd forms of ammunition. Their selection of other weapons might be considered sparse by some, but when it comes to bolts, arrows, and more exotic ranged projectiles, they are unmatched. Magical ammunition, as well as trick-arrows and other oddities, may be available here.
4: Famous Smith	This weaponsmith is famous for a particularly skilled or infamous individual smith who may or may not still work there. Items that bear the mark of the smith would be treated with special reverence, and their bearers given special privileges.
5: Famous Weapon	This weaponsmith is famous for a particular sword, axe, or polearm that may or may not have been crafted there. The famous item is present, either protected away or on clear display. It is valuable, and perhaps even magical, but well-known throughout the region.
6: Famous Armor	This weaponsmith is famous for a particular shield, helm, or suit of armor that may or may not have been crafted there. The famous item is present, either protected away or on clear display. It is valuable, and perhaps even magical, but well-known throughout the region.
7: Ex-Criminal	This weaponsmith has a history; their skills with the sword and the hammer have not always been put to the best use, but that is behind them now. They may be trying to escape their past, hide from it, or redeem themselves with good, hard work.

Weaponsmith Quirk	Description
8: Quartermaster	This weaponsmith is affiliated with the local military outfit, and is bitter about being stuck behind with the grunt work of outfitting other soldiers (and paying customers) with arms and armor. They may have orders not to deal with outsiders under specific circumstances.
9: Mender	This weaponsmith is a scavenger who specializes in restoring broken weapons back to new quality; or, more often, making a new weapon out of the parts of many other hopeless weapons. They cannot help but speculate at interesting item "combinations," and will happily buy weapon-related scrap and garbage from the characters.
10: Monster Hater	This weaponsmith despises a particular kind of monster or supernatural being. If they believe the characters are likely to hunt or fight the subject of their hatred, they would be inclined to offer discounts, as well as access to special items.
11: Estranged	Something makes this weaponsmith different from the rest of their community. Their intelligence, foreign nature, or noble upbringing sets them apart and may make them more empathetic to traveling characters from another land. They will not hesitate to give inside information and frank opinions about the town.
12: Connections	This weaponsmith has current, active connections with the local criminals, gangs, or thieves' guild. They are most likely a supplier or arms smuggler, or a fence for stolen goods. Either way, the characters may become embroiled in intrigue, accidentally or intentionally, spending too much time or coin there.
13: Retired	This weaponsmith was once an adventurer but has since given up a life of travel and outdoor camping in favor of a more calm, sedate living. They may be aging out of the weaponsmithing game as well. For either fighting or crafting, the characters will need to persuade this smith to take up the hammer again.
14: Inventor	This weaponsmith in an innovator, currently developing the next stage of weaponcraft in their society. Whether this is firearms, advanced siege engines, flying machines, forms of magical destruction, or clockwork devices, the characters have the chance to be on the cutting edge of technology.
15: Collector	This weaponsmith was once a great traveler and appreciates the opportunity to add a trophy to their collection. Body parts collected from exotic or strange animals, beasts, and monsters may earn characters discounts on their weapons, or the opportunity to trade for another item from the collection.

Weaponsmith Quirk	Description
16: Prophet	This weaponsmith has a strange or spooky knack for foretelling the future and knowing exactly what kind of weapon a character is going to need later in their career. The vision is rarely clear, and the choice of weapon does not always reveal the nature of the upcoming threat, but the prophet is rarely wrong.
17: Secretive	This weaponsmith has concern, justified or not, that their community might frown upon them dealing with outsiders like the characters. They still want to buy and sell with the characters, but attempt to do so secretly while still maintaining a facade of public refusal.
18: Undersupplied	This weaponsmith can craft what the characters need; their only problem is that they can't build it right now. Their lack of supplies may stem from unjust blacklisting within the local guild system, or the weaponsmith is simply not well-liked or not good at their job. They complain constantly about their lack of supplies being the only thing holding them back.
19: Metallurgist	This weaponsmith was a former miner-turned-metallurgist, and knows their way around various metals and alloys with great expertise. They are the ideal choice for handling complex or exotic metal components.
20: Savant	This weaponsmith has difficulty explaining themselves clearly to others, but their work is unparalleled in the land. Although their reputation for quality is well-known, patrons rarely get more than a vague idea what the final piece will look like before the artist has completed it.

Prison Quirks (d20)

Certain characters might get thrown in prison more than once—some characters might even become quite familiar with each prison in a given town or region, able to discuss the pros and cons of living within, and breaking out of, different jails and lockups. Roll here to add some spice and make a given prison feel unique and special.

Prison Quirk	Description
1: Leaky	This prison is not just damp and dank, it is downright moist. Mold and lichen of all sorts grow in the cells, as well as odd, potentially poisonous toadstools. Puddles form in inconvenient places and disease is inevitable—but the water damage to the structure may have created some unexpected avenues of escape.
2: Pitch Black	This prison offers no light sources in its windowless halls. The guards may be equipped with lanterns, but if so, these are the only lights in the entire facility. Security measures include simple tricks that exploit the blindness of anyone trying to navigate their way to freedom.
3: Pitted	This prison is riddled with pits as a security measure. These pits might be few in number, but cunningly concealed; alternatively, they may be featured at every intersection, presenting more of a mobility and logistical challenge to would-be escapees.
4: High Perch	This prison has been built at the summit of some deep precipice—such as on a mountaintop or over a deep chasm. Prisoners can be (and regularly are) neatly disposed of by a window or other opening, either through legal or "unofficial" execution.
5: Featureless	This prison is unnervingly featureless. All of the walls, floors, doors, and other surfaces are the same featureless color, and the whole place is disturbingly clean. This disquieting atmosphere causes many prisoners to lose their grip on reality.
6: Violent	This prison is especially prone to violence between prisoners. The guards may be especially lax in security or uninterested in breaking up fights, or perhaps the prisoners themselves are especially agitated due to prison conditions or other factors.
7: Brutal	This prison is especially prone to violence inflicted by the guards upon the prisoners. Perhaps the guards have been instructed by a particularly harsh policy or leader, or simply have a penchant for cruelty themselves. Either way, even minor infractions by prisoners will incur swift and malicious punishment.

Prison Quirk	Description
8: Guard Beasts	This prison is notorious for having well-trained beasts (or a specific beast or kind of beast) as a main security feature. These may be mundane animals like dogs, bears, tigers, etc., or supernatural monsters like hell hounds or dragons. The beasts are not necessarily as intelligent as their human counterparts, but have training and wits beyond that of typical members of their species.
9: All-Seeing	This prison has been equipped with the means to monitor prisoners, either through magical "cameras" or more mundane means such as privacy-removing architecture, mirrors, and spies among the guards and/or prisoners. The prisoners know they are being watched, which has rendered them hopeless and apathetic.
10: Automated	Many of the systems of this prison, ranging from how the prisoners are guarded to how they are released from their cells or fed, are automated for the prison's ease and to cut back on staffing. This may mean that literal automatons or magical machines perform the tasks, or that mechanisms in the prison architecture handle them. Alternatively, the guards and staff might just be so robotic and detached from their duties that they may as well be machines.
11: Hard Labor	The inmates of this prison are forced to labor for hours on end at a task either on premises or nearby. The labor may range from mining coal or salt to smelting and forging weapons for the local lord. A prison requiring more specialized labor might encourage the town guard to focus on arresting certain skillful individuals in greater numbers.
12: Honorable Prisoners	This prison has somehow managed to cultivate a culture of honor amongst the inmates. They generally police themselves, keep order, and solve any disputes through organized boxing matches. This dynamic may have been started by the prisoners themselves or somehow enforced by the wardens.
13: Unbearable Temperature	This prison is either insufferably cold or boiling hot. It may even swing between those two extremes! But it is never, ever comfortable. Prisoners here are always in states of severe exhaustion and misery due to these conditions.
14: Starved Prisoners	This prison refuses inmates full meals, perhaps starving them for days or even weeks at a time. This keeps the prisoners weak, but also makes them savage and desperate. Starved prisoners are just as likely to turn on each other as they are to try to escape; but whoever has the food, has the power.

Prison Quirk	Description
15: Unsavory Disposal	This prison secretly turns the bodies and organs of deceased prisoners over to criminals, the black market, or otherwise disreputable individuals. What happens to these bodies is anyone's guess—and even if the wardens think they know, they probably neither have, nor desire, the full details of the arrangement.
16: Solid Hierarchy	This prison has a well-organized and well-known hierarchy of inmates. The leader at the top of the hierarchy might be the strongest, smartest, or simply the most ruthless criminal of the lot, or they might not; but since no one questions their superiors in the chain of command, there are rarely any coups.
17: Secret Experiments	This prison runs operations and experiments upon its inmates in secret. These experiments might be to develop incredible new abilities in test subjects, or to perfect some new magic or weapon, or simply to learn more about the anatomy of the prisoners for research purposes. The prisoners who know about the experiments are helpless to stop them.
18: Friendly	Everyone is just really, really nice and easygoing in the prison—guards, prisoners, even the chef and gardener all seem like they enjoy being there. They all agree that it's a nice, refreshing change from a typical prison, and there is no greater mystery to it, despite what the characters might think.
19: Hidden	The location of this prison is not common knowledge, not even to the inmates imprisoned there. Those who escape, or who try to rescue those who have been sent to this prison, will have to contend with solving the mystery of where they are first.
20: Psychic Trap	This prison has additional features (supernatural or otherwise), which allow it to control and limit the prisoners, not just physically, but psychically as well. These methods could vary in intensity from defeatist messages and artwork to outright magical illusions, mind control, or nightmare hallucinations designed to break the will of the inmates.

Temple Quirks (d20)

The gods help those who help themselves. But sometimes the best way for a character to help themselves is by visiting the gods at home to plead their case. Every church and shrine is different; roll here to add character to the next place of worship that they visit.

Temple Quirk	Description
1: Artistic	Beautiful artwork (stained glass, wood, or marble carvings, etc.) decorates many of the surfaces of this temple. The beauty of this place is obvious to everyone, but quite fragile; it would be easy for an enemy of the church to target.
2: Reliquary	This temple contains the remains of a famous saint or holy person within the faith. The dust and bones are contained in a precious vessel, likely below ground, and may actually possess great spiritual powers.
3: Protected	Specific kinds of supernatural beings are unable to enter the walls of this temple. These wardings may cause trouble when they indiscriminately target one of the characters for some reason.
4: Portentous	Something unusual about this temple—its size, shape, location, material, or dogma—is the product of a prophecy. The temple's builder believed that following this strange requirement would fulfill the prophecy.
5: Library	This temple holds a wealth of old texts related to the faith. Ancient omens, lost histories, and dire truths might be uncovered by delving into the dustiest tomes, or a book itself might be found to be of great spiritual value.
6: Dream Inducing	A well-known rumor, that those who sleep within the walls of the temple experience visions from a god, turns out to be true. But there is some reason for the god's communication in this particular place.
7: Thin Veil	This temple was built in a place where the boundaries between the worlds are thin. Perhaps souls, demons, angels, or other entities can cross over into the mortal world here, or vice versa.
8: Well-Armed	This temple is well-stocked with arms and armor, either for the purposes of defending the temple, keeping order in town, or persecuting the unfaithful. The clergy all know how to use them.
9: Wild	Whether dedicated to a nature deity or not, this temple is overgrown with either animals (pets, guardians, or local fauna) and plants (vines, mold, trees). The faithful care for the wildlife as part of the temple.
10: Humble	The simple appearance of this temple belies its importance to the community of the faithful. Whether due to age or historical importance, the lack of decoration hides an unsurpassed devotion.

Temple Quirk	Description
11: Squalid	The charity work provided by this temple has left it noticeably unhygienic and crowded. The hundreds of poor who make use of the services here might slow down characters or make them uncomfortable.
12: Unnatural Weather	The sky above this temple is always blessed with weather that seems to reflect the aesthetics of the faith rather than the weather of the town at large.
13: Benevolently Damaged	A part of this temple has been destroyed and never repaired, due to the belief that the god of the temple chose to smite said portion and wishes it to remain thusly destroyed. The clergy are horrified at any suggestions to repair the damage.
14: Charismatic	The clergy of this temple are especially friendly and convincing in their evangelical sales pitches. Their charming attitude might be sincere or hide dishonest motives.
15: Miraculous	A miracle is either purported to have occurred here, or else continues to occur here. The miraculous object or person might be hidden away or on display for the faithful to bear witness.
16: Ostentatious	This temple's outrageous displays of wealth are outright provocative to any would-be robbers. The security is commensurately large, well-equipped, and zealous.
17: Ossuary	This temple doesn't just have a graveyard, or a mere crypt. Thousands upon thousands of skeletons fill the chambers below the structure, perhaps even spilling out into the church proper.
18: Heretical	This temple worships an alternative version of the religion that it purports to profess. The main body of the faith might tolerate this offshoot branch, or actively persecute it.
19: Secret	The existence of this temple is generally known only to the faithful or those who are considered close friends. This may be out of necessity, or simply a dramatic or symbolic choice of the faithful.
20: Sacred Words	The deity of this temple has in some manner communicated a divine message through or upon it, either through writing (upon an altar or wall) or word (a sacred place where the voice of the deity, or an oracle, can be heard).

Warden Quirks (d20)

A hardened criminal who knows their way around prisons will tell you—the warden always has their own agenda. When a criminal is attempting a breakout, the temperament and behavior of the warden can play a huge role in hindering (or furthering) those plans. Roll here to see what kind of a warden is in charge of the local prison.

Warden Quirk	Description
1: Cruel	This warden is needlessly and sadistically cruel to the inmates under their control. Their desire is to break the spirits of everyone in the prison, either through torture, control, or other more inventive punishments.
2: Kind	This warden takes a more caring and compassionate attitude to the inmates in their care. Their desire is to make everyone in the prison as comfortable and happy as possible while still adhering to protocol when unavoidable.
3: Sympathetic	This warden, while not a pushover, is in some way sympathetic to the inmates' plight—maybe a result of being a former criminal or prisoner themselves. Their desire is to avoid the mistakes that other wardens have made, now that they are in the position of power.
4: Pragmatic	This warden is a practical thinker who tries to look at things from a detached position; they are willing to listen to prisoners if they have good arguments and sound logic. Their desire is to keep the prison running smoothly, even if the old ways need to be changed.
5: Warrior	This warden was, and still is, a mighty combatant who rules the jail with their own iron fist, often meting out inmate punishments personally. Their desire is to prove, through direct action, their combat prowess over all of the inmates, so as to clarify their role as "top dog." No one has been able to beat them yet.
6: Corrupt	This warden is deep in the pockets of some influential nobles, criminals, or other nefarious individuals. Their desire is to make as much money as they possibly can while concealing the nature of their corruption.
7: Philosopher	This warden believes that they have come to a new understanding about the politics, ethics, or economics of running the prison. Their desire is to restructure the prison to fit their vision of the future.
8: Dark Allegiances	This warden is not just corrupt; they have connections that would mark them as a traitor, heretic, or outright monster to their fellow citizens. Their desire is to use the inmates left at their mercy as resources to further the agendas of their dark masters.

Warden Quirk	Description
9: Parental	This warden takes a decidedly creepy attitude of "parental guidance" toward their inmates, whom they treat like wayward children who need to be corrected. Their desire is to maintain the sick illusion that they are a caring and beloved (if occasionally stern) parent rather than a warden.
10: Deformed	This warden is rumored to be horribly marred in their appearance and is never seen directly. Their desire is to continue to conceal the truth of this rumor and allow their legend to grow beyond the reality as a way to rule through fear.
11: Bureaucratic	This warden is focused on following the letter of every law, rule, and regulation that the prison has. Their desire is to keep everything official and proper, with less regard for whether the jail is actually running properly.
12: Playful	This warden does not take their role terribly seriously. Rather than use their power over the inmates toward cruel or ambitious ends, this warden's desire is only to play pranks, have fun, and generally spread chaos throughout the prison.
13: Sporting	This warden is obsessed with physical competitions and often pits prisoners against each other in elaborate matches. The nature of the sporting events might not always be violent, but they are always dangerous for the inmates.
14: Religious	This warden is a devout worshipper of a particular local religion or deity. Their desire may be to answer the calling of their faith by converting the inmates under their watch, or offering more compassionate, redemptive oversight.
15: Dramatic	This warden is driven by their emotions and often responds to situations impulsively rather than rationally. Their desire is to express themselves and make sure that they appear to be doing a good job, regardless of the truth of the issue.
16: Distracted	This warden is preoccupied with some business, hobby, or relationship outside of the typical duties of running the prison. Their desire is to pursue this other venture, to the detriment of their job.
17: Lecherous	This warden might be seeking carnal pleasure or an actual life partner; either way, they have no problems with abusing their power and authority as a way to pressure inmates and other citizens into getting what they want.
18: Well-Armed	This warden keeps a wide assortment of weapons and ammunition in their own personal offices, rather than the guard posts or armories of the prison. This may save them, or backfire wildly if the inmates ever gained access to said offices.

Warden Quirk	Description
19: Cursed	This warden, whether in fact or merely in their own mind, has inherited a family curse. The prison itself may be tied to this curse or merely serve as an effective symbol of the burden they carry.
20: Creature of the Night	This warden is not human, but masquerades as one. Their supernatural nature makes them more effective at their duties, while being a warden grants them access to victims.

Criminals (d20)

Sometimes the characters are subject to the predations of ill-willed folk. Maybe the character has, intentionally or otherwise, made themselves vulnerable; adventurers are juicy targets, after all. Roll here to see what manner of criminals are nearby.

Criminal	Description
1: Pickpocket	A classic vagabond disguise helps this individual, quite possibly a child, to hide in a crowd. This thief may work as an individual, or as part of a larger gang, and aims for items that will not be noticed until long after the theft.
2: Smuggler	For good or ill, this person makes their money trafficking in some goods deemed illegal (or highly taxable) in the land. They may view the characters as potential buyers or sellers of their goods; or more likely, they might view the characters as potential witting or unwitting mules to transport the goods.
3: Dark Wizard	Corrupted by foul magic, this wizard is up to something. And whether it's collecting bodies, harvesting illegal spell components, or simply yearning for one of the character's magic items, it's not going to end on nice terms.
4: Spy for Local Lord	The government has planted this spy to sniff out any dissent or dissatisfaction amongst the populace. They may be quiet and go unnoticed or be rather obtuse in their investigation of any outspoken individuals.
5: Spy for Local Criminals	A thieves guild or gang has placed this spy to look out for their interests. This includes pinpointing outsiders who might interfere with guild plans. The spy will probably go unnoticed; but be prepared to roll several more times on this chart as more and more guild agents follow the spy's tip.
6: Spy for Local Monster	A monster native to the region has hired a local outcast to spy upon their community. The monster might be anything; perhaps a dragon or some other intelligent and powerful beast, or a tribe of goblins, orcs, or lizardfolk.
7: Murderer	This thief has no regard for life and will try to earn their coin by plunging a knife into the neck of the first character whom they think they can kill and rob. They may be desperate, or simply ruthless, but they are not necessarily skilled at their craft.
8: Violent Drunk	This person's only crime may be the belligerent attitude they take on when they drink; however, right now, they are just drunk enough to pick a fight with anyone and anything. There is no reasoning with the drunk, but other forms of clever persuasion are not out of the question.

Criminal	Description
9: Acrobatic Thief	This thief relies on their quick reflexes, rather than pure stealth, to pull off their crime. They will wait for the chance to create an "accident" that conceals their nimble theft or try to get close enough to their target to grab a valuable item and run.
10: Ambusher	This criminal won't hesitate to resort to violence immediately, targeting solo travelers whenever possible. They will try to take down weak-looking individuals quickly and quietly, to then immediately pull any and all accessible items off of their bodies.
11: Intolerant Inquisitor	This representative of a harsh and zealous faith has viewed the characters with condemnation for some perceived sin. They will seek vengeance and some form of atonement for the heresy.
12: Mugger	This thief will state their business first: to relieve wanderers of their coin. The characters are given a chance to hand over a stated amount of gold, or else all of their gold and treasure, or else their horses and the clothes on their back too. Talking can easily make things worse.
13: Hired Bounty Hunter	Someone was mad enough to hire a bounty hunter to capture one of the characters, theoretically, alive. Whomever is the villain who hired them, the bounty hunter is entirely neutral in motive. This is just a paycheck, but they do take pride in their work.
14: Overambitious Corpse-Looter	This scavenger has gotten a mind that the characters are high-risk investments; and when they die, this looter wants to be there to pick the bones clean. They might not be subtle about their spying, to the point that they may eventually try to facilitate the transition to corpsehood ahead of schedule.
15: Con Artist	A swindler has marked the characters as the perfect victims to participate in a set of classic rigged games, or hear a desperate plea that conceals a lie beneath. Figuring out the con is fairly easy, but what the characters do about it could become complicated.
16: Trained Assassin	Someone, or something, has marked the characters for death. This professional has studied their targets well and knows all of their abilities, every trick and spell that has been made public knowledge. They have prepared for a showdown and will wait for the right moment to strike.
17: Pirate	This robber is prone to attacking vessels at sea; on land, they are less confident in their authority. Nonetheless, old habits die hard, and a cutlass and hooked hand hurt just as well whether on- or off-deck. The pirate may bluster and make grand demands but is probably just very drunk.

Criminal	Description
18: Spellsneak	This individual is either a wizard gone rogue or a thief who has picked up some magical competence. Either way, they use their magical talents of invisibility, charming, distraction, and a bit of telekinesis to try to relieve the characters of their magical goods.
19: Honeypot	This seducer has the intention to learn the desires of the characters, whatever they may be, and use them to get the characters into a compromised position where robbing them is easier. Alternatively, monstrous forces are using the honeypot to lure victims out of town.
20: Monster	This criminal is truly a creature of the night; quite literally, it is some manner of vampire, shadow-beast, or other nightmarish horror. It might be local to the region or a visitor. It might be an individual or one of many lurking behind closed doors.

Villains (d20)

Some individuals in town are evil but remain at large despite what evidence may have been gathered against them. Villains are too clever, powerful, or well-connected to be taken down by ordinary means. Heroes who would seek to defeat them will have to be smart enough to avoid getting arrested in the process.

Villain	Description
1: Cultist	This villain is a devotee of dark and forbidden powers. They can be defeated by exposing their crimes and strange, occult rituals to the public, who will immediately want them burned at the stake.
2: Crime Boss	This villain is the leader of a crime syndicate or gang. They can be defeated by convincing the town guard to stop taking their bribes, or with sheer force (the guards won't cover for them once they are dead).
3: Monstrous Predator	This villain may hide among the populace, but they are, in actuality, a creature or monster of some kind. They can be defeated by tracking them back to their lair or ambushing them during an attack on a victim.
4: Shapeshifter	This villain has the ability to change their appearance and disguise themselves as anybody. They can be defeated by deducing their pattern of aliases or discovering how to expose their true form.
5: Influencer	This villain is simply extremely talented at charming, manipulating, and otherwise controlling people in town. They can be defeated by figuring out what blackmail they have against key individuals in town or by somehow turning their "friends" against them.
6: Dark Merchant	This villain achieves their goals through mercantile savvy, providing the underworld elements in town with illicit smuggled goods in return for safety. They can be defeated by finding and cutting their supply lines or discovering and eliminating the criminals who harbor them.
7: Corrupt Noble	This villain is a member of high society and remains untouchable so long as their reputation holds. They can be defeated by exposing (with rock-solid evidence) their well-hidden ties and criminal contacts.
8: Unbeatable Warrior	This villain is a champion who, thus far, has remained undefeated by every warrior in town. The town guard has given up on trying to stop them. They can be defeated by finally besting them in combat, either through greater strength or clever trickery.
9: Bounty Hunter	This villain is a hunter of people, selling their skills to the highest bidder without moral qualms. They can be defeated by a hunter who can get one step ahead of their hunting strategy.

Villain	Description
10: Enemy Soldier	This villain is a skilled warrior in an enemy military organization, but due to fear of reprisals, no one will touch them. They can be defeated by posing as another faction and letting them take the heat for the attack.
11: Anarch Terrorist	This villain hides amongst the populace, planning attacks upon the town from within. They can be defeated by deducing their anarchist motives based on their chosen targets.
12: Evil Magician	This villain is a practitioner of powerful secret arts, and through these talents has managed to hide the evidence of their evil deeds. They can be defeated by destroying the magical items that power and conceal their magic.
13: Cursed Citizen	This villain is a townsperson who was born with, or permanently transformed into, a terrifying appearance. The easiest way to "defeat" them is to extend them the compassion they have been denied by other townsfolk.
14: Trickster	This villain is dedicated not to the pursuit of evil, but pure mischief. They can be defeated by putting up a "merry chase" and letting them play their game to completion.
15: Intelligent Item	This villain may have once been mortal but now is actually a sentient item, weapon, or artifact of some kind. They can be defeated by learning how to undo the magic that binds them to the item.
16: Disguised Deity	This villain is able to take the form of a mortal, but they are in fact a god in disguise (or at least the avatar of one). They can be defeated only by fulfilling their specific duty (after which they will leave the mortals to their devices), or by being driven away with powerful enough magic from an opposing deity.
17: Twisted Inventor	This villain conceals themself as a simple inventor, but in reality their genius has been twisted toward evil deeds. They can be defeated by destroying the power source or control mechanism for their host of dark inventions.
18: Rival Industrialist	This villain poses as an ordinary business person in town, but in truth their cutthroat tactics have cost the town dearly. They can be defeated by business rivals who are willing to go even more cutthroat than they are, or who will rewrite the rules of the game, just as they have done.
19: Monstrous Leader	This villain may be a monster or a townsperson; either way, they have somehow become the leader of a group of monsters, whom they can sneak into town regularly. They can be defeated by finding and securing the route which the leader uses to allow their forces entry to town.
20: Evil Genius	This villain always outthinks their foes, staying three steps ahead at all times. They can be defeated by discovering the one emotional attachment that makes them act irrationally.

Prisoners (d20)

Characters might end up in a town prison for any number of deserved or undeserved reasons. They are unlikely to be the only prisoner in their cell, let alone the prison; roll here to find out what other prisoners they might be locked up alongside, either as potential allies or enemies in any attempts they make to escape!

Prisoner	Description
1: Devrick Lennimon	Devrick is a member of the local thieves guild, but a quick assessment of his skills or history in the guild reveals the truth—he is the worst thief who ever had the misfortune of bearing the title.
2: Gylin Danford	Gylin was thrown in jail for evading payments to his local lord (tax evasion) and firmly believes that his guilt does not make him a criminal like all the other common inmates.
3: Kidya Mardowell	Kidya was an apprentice to a well-known inventor in the region, until she and many of her friends were arrested for accidental damages caused by one of their collective inventions.
4: Zara Hayward	Zara is a specialist, ironically, in breaking into prisons, the crime for which she has been interred here. She is well aware that breaking out of prisons has thus far proven to be much more difficult a feat than getting into them ever was.
5: Nomrin Blaskirr	Nomrin was a loyal soldier who carried out a job for a local lord. What he did not know was that he had been set up as the fall-man for the lord's schemes, and now wants vengeance.
6: Dwyll Darannow	Dwyll is a hard-on-his-luck burglar who stole to feed his family one too many times. He sees the error of his ways, but not how to better his lot, none of which will matter when he is hanged in a week's time.
7: Jim Blacktongue	Jim is a prisoner who seems physically incapable of being honest. He lies for reasons that make no sense, and lies even when he has nothing to gain. He will probably introduce himself to the party as "Barney."
8: Andrew Uldumhill	Andrew was locked up under suspicion of dark magic or immoral experimentation. Whether he is an evil mastermind or a benevolent genius is anyone's guess.
9: Jasper	Jasper was a captured soldier of an enemy army, or a particular aggressive bandit gang. He hates the town and everyone in it, including the other prisoners, unless convinced to see them as potential allies.

Prisoner	Description
10: Scryne	Scryne is a short scholar with a glass eye who was locked up for "knowing too much." This knowledge might be dark, forbidden lore; or it might simply be incriminating evidence that the powers-that-be want to suppress.
11: Garthak'k the Brutal	This barbarian is from out of town and doesn't know the local customs—although he does know when he's being insulted. Unfortunately, when people make him feel stupid, he tends to lash out, which is how he ended up in prison.
12: Catsey	Catsey is a straw-haired little sneak thief and pickpocket who was given many chances back in society—nine lives, if you will—before the town guard finally got sick of him. Catsey feels bad, but even if freed, will never turn from his true love: stealing.
13: Jessica Harken	Jessica is an unrepentant thief and seductress who will happily betray her fellow prisoners for a chance at freedom or riches—all the while playing the part of the damsel in distress.
14: Carla Windmar	Carla is a murderess with a string of bodies to her name—far more than any one town would know about. Her reign of terror will continue in the prison if extra care is not taken to keep weapons and cutlery far out of her capable reach.
15: Aidalanthia Brown	Aida is a blonde woman with a reason to look nervous: one of the prison guards is obsessively in love with her. While she is actually a thief, his plan to "redeem" her has led her to hide away a knife under her tunic, just in case.
16: Martha Mayfair	Martha is an older mute woman with a young babe wailing in her arms. She has been placed in prison for "vagrancy," but has difficulty communicating that this is just the guard's way of providing her and the child with a dry place to lie for the night. She resists any attempts to be freed.
17: Marlowe Sevenbreath	Marlowe was a bard at some point in his career, but his never-still tongue got him in trouble in one too many noble courts. He means well but, because he never stops talking, will inevitably rub a character the wrong way if given enough time.
18: Wendy Strongbow	Wendy and her husband were indentured servants who attempted to flee their master to find work in another town. They were caught, and now Wendy (perhaps without her husband for some reason) is on her way to be sent back to the lord who owns their debt.
19: Heathcliff	Heathcliff has gone stark raving mad, no doubt the ultimate reason for his imprisonment. He believes that he has been given the gift of prophecy by some god, which may or may not be true.
20: Sarah Cardenfield	Sarah claims to have been arrested for accidentally trespassing on a noble's land. In reality, she works for the nobility, particularly the nobles who run the prison, and spies for the guards.

Gangs (d20)

When characters get on the wrong side of the law, long-term problems can arise, and sometimes the law itself is the least of their concerns. Roll here if you need a quick-and-ready gang to spring on the party as villains, unlikely allies, or just local color.

Gang	Description
1: The Dead Snake League	This gang nails a small serpent to the door of their enemies as a threat to not cross them. Most people fear the symbol more than they do the gang, partially due to the penchant locals have for using the dead snake symbol against their neighbors over petty quarrels. Animal vendors can't seem to stock enough garden snakes to suit local needs.
2: The Harvesters	This gang of former farmers, rangers, and others from the nearby wilderness are paying the city back for perceived crimes against the rural community and/or nature. They revisit the pain inflicted upon animals and plants upon those most guilty.
3: The Demolishers	A gang notorious for targeting buildings for arson or other forms of destruction. Their motives may be anarchic, thievery-based, or simple gleeful madness. Alternatively, the town may have individuals who provide something called "insurance."
4: The Fools	Though they chose their own name to match their harlequin-like masks, this gang did not expect their title to be so apt. The only thing this gang can manage to accomplish is providing comic relief.
5: The Throatless Circle	Known for their literal and figurative silence, the Circle are unmatched in their ruthlessness. Their membership almost exclusively consists of sociopaths and others who have rejected their fellow citizens.
6: Maggie's Mashers	Maggie leads her gang, known for a preference toward fisticuffs and improvised knuckle-guards over other weapons, with an iron grip. The gang follows certain traditions, most of which revolve around one-on-one combat.
7: The Grim Seven	Each of the seven members of this gang specializes in a different skill or talent. They all have a common origin however: a sad event that led to the initial formation of the gang.
8: The Knights	A noble but militant gang who look out for their own. They follow a code of conduct that binds them into an uneasy alliance with other gangs and criminal factions in town. Some of these other factions do not hold this same sense of honor among thieves, and exploit their knowledge of the Knights' code of conduct to twist it against them.

Gang	Description
9: The House of Mysteries	This gang focuses on the acquisition of rare, exotic, or supernatural items. Their numbers are few, but they are all specialists in the art of the heist. Their headquarters is especially difficult to locate, as they meet in the backroom of an ordinary shop. Their vault, however, is in a faraway location that only the gang members know about.
10: The Natives	This gang has formed and grown around some perceived argument with a group of new arrivals in town. The Natives have lived in town longer than this new competition, and focus on this narrative of cultural ownership as a way to enforce their territorial claim and keep their coffers full.
11: The New Blood	This gang formed around the need to defend a particular minority group, or several minority groups in town, from crime-related problems. The New Blood have been at least partly responsible for high tensions between themselves and other local, more entrenched gangs, and the threat of a gang war always seems to loom closer every year.
12: The Chained Blades	This gang maintains close ties to agents within the local prison, to the point that they functionally control the prisons (and much of the local judicial system as a result). Characters who cross the Blades should be wary of being sent to prison, as they may find their sentence unexpectedly lengthened.
13: The Black Coffers	A gang with deep connections to the city watch. They have enough corrupted officers of the law on their side to sway other criminals to their cause and control which crime is permitted in town. Characters who cross them will find that neither side of the law is safe for them.
14: The Kind Men	A small, poor gang that, by virtue of having won the hearts and minds of a disenfranchised neighborhood, has the resources of the entire neighborhood to fall back upon when necessary. They are, nonetheless, ruthless killers who wield this power to their full strategic advantage against enemies.
15: The Hollow Marksmen	A gang of assassins who specialize in vengeance-based killings. They kill the victim in plain sight and either escape or die, so as to let the town know that it was Vengeance who killed the victim and thereby honor their mysterious faith. They can be hired to execute a killing on a character's behalf, but proof of a genuine grievance must be presented.
16: The Fiery Wave	A community of artists, perhaps with one particular visionary "prophet" at the center of the movement, is the heart of this gang. They graffiti the town with their symbols, iconography, and aesthetics while committing petty crime against institutions that they vocally protest.

Gang	Description
17: The Rum Runners	This gang specializes in smuggling all kinds of goods; rum is hardly their only commodity. Although they are not willing to give a full list of what they have transported into and out of city limits, there is, in reality, little that they are not willing to move for the right price.
18: The Hidden Hands	A gang of weapons dealers. A potential customer needs to know the right gang code words, but if they do, then they have access to some highly illegal weapons, poisons, and other instruments of death.
19: Cirque de Slay	This gang is a masquerade of mischief and crime. They regularly throw parties to which all locals are invited, but most are too afraid to attend. Their celebrations are dangerous and incredible all at once, and their performances provide a night to remember.
20: The Shadow-Folk	Specializing in secrecy and stealth, this gang is unique in that it is not a gang at all, but rather an individual who has, through magic or other mischief, managed to be in two places at once. Their ability allows them to carry out large-scale crimes with precise coordination.

Livestock (d20)

Visiting local farms and villages, and even just traveling around a typical town, one is likely to see their share of livestock. Such animals might be found in fields, pens, or even large carts (inside, or pulling them). Roll here to see what kind of livestock are found.

1: Cow

2: Steer/Cattle

3: Yaks

4: Oxen

5: Aurochs

6: Workhorses

7: Riding Horses

8: Ponies

9: Donkeys

10: Mules

11: Sheep

12: Lambs

13: Goats

14: Pigs

15: Chickens

16: Turkeys/Geese (or other fowl)

17: Bees

18: Llamas/Alpacas

19: Rabbits

20: Talking Animals

Pets (d20)

The human inhabitants of many homes, businesses, and tradeshops in town might call an animal or two among their own. Small animals like these could live indoors and might guard while the human occupants are absent. Roll here to see what kind of pet might be found in a particular home or structure.

1: Tiny Lapdog

2: Small Dog

3: Hunting Dog

4: Big Boy Dog

5: Skinny Cat

6: Fat Cat

7: Old Scraggly Cat

8: Hawk/Falcon

9: Barn Owl

10: Turtle Dove

11: Sparrow/Songbird

12: Raven/Crow

13: Serpent

14: Rabbit

15: Toad

16: Parrot

17: Mastiff/War Hound

18: Badger

19: Monkey

20: Magical Beast/Familiar

Vermin (d20)

One constant of any town: where enough people congregate, so too do the vermin. If adventurers go seeking the source of a plague or if the inn has suddenly been shut down due to health code violations, roll here to see what nearby infestation is responsible.

1: Rats

2: House/Field Mice

3: Cockroaches

4: Spiders

5: Beetles

6: Raccoons

7: Ticks

8: Ants

9: Weasels

10: Bees/Wasps

11: Gnats

12: Snakes

13: Flies/Mosquitos

14: Frogs/Toads

15: Termites

16: Fleas

17: Earwigs/Silverfish

18: Bats

19: Locusts

20: Sentient Worms

Cults (d20)

Any community large enough for mainstream religion will also give birth to its share of heretical offshoots, grassroots movements, and other cults. Creepy cults are a staple of life in any town, and it doesn't always matter which cult made a particular piece of ancient treasure or built the local temple on a font of magical energy. Roll here to generate an on-the-fly random cult for your town.

Cult	Description
1: Fish/Ocean Cult	Centered around a sea god, monster, or other underwater entity of some kind. Imagery: spirals, octopoids, tentacles, fins, waves and islands.
2: Demon Cult	Follows the will of demons or other evil spiritual entities. Imagery: bat wings, fanged and grinning faces, skulls, scenes of torment, fire.
3: Angel Cult	Follows the will of angels or other good spiritual entities. Imagery: white feathers, androgynous silhouettes, choral/tinkling music, shafts of light, halos.
4: Dragon Cult	Worships a dragon or dragons in general. Imagery: draconic forms, robed cultists, dragon skulls, dragons at war/ruling, humans bowing down.
5: Death Cult	Follows a god that personifies death. Imagery: skulls, bones, graves/tombs, the underworld, souls in transit.
6: Political Cult	Centered around a particular political movement or individual. Imagery: images of the town, scenes from the town, images of leaders and famous individuals, seal of the city.
7: Witch/Coven Cult	Made up of witches, or follows the will of a single witch or coven. Imagery: the moon(s), herbs, divination cards, alchemical symbols, animals.
8: Magician's Cult	Studies the work of a particular magician: either firsthand (if they are still living and teaching), or through their work and texts. Imagery: alchemical symbols, magician's personal rune, books/tomes, astrological symbols.
9: Nature Cult	Worships nature in all its forms, either in cooperation with, or in antagonism against, civilization and the town. Imagery: vegetation, trees, animal heads, heavenly bodies, caves.
10: Dark God's Cult	Worships a malicious and evil god or entity. Imagery: eyes, jagged crowns, dark towers, gauntlets, chains.
11: Dark Goddess's Cult	Worships a cruel and evil goddess or entity. Imagery: orbs, crystals, rod/whip, chalice of blood, dark flowers.

Cult	Description
12: Hidden Deity's Cult	Worships a secret deity whose true nature is concealed from the world. Imagery: empty cup, fingers in "secret" position, covered/broken mirrors, mustard seeds, blindfold.
13: Assassin's Cult	Participates in ritual murder and other violent traditions. Imagery: daggers, skulls, hooded figures, shut eyes, white flowers.
14: Lost/Forgotten Deity's Cult	Worships a deity whose true nature is lost to the world. Imagery: religious iconography with strange, almost heretical twists.
15: Transcendental Cult	Seeks to ascend beyond their mortal forms. Imagery: the "new world," the "ascent," their "new forms," the leader/lead entity.
16: Labor/Wealth Cult	Centered around the acquisition of wealth or a common profession amongst its members. Imagery: coins, currency, hammers, working folks, local lords.
17: Paladin/ Knightly Order	Centered around an order of knights who held power and influence in the region. The Knights may have guarded a dark secret. Imagery: coats of arms, knights at attention, knights in battle, enemies of the knights.
18: Regional Cult (Natural region)	Dedicated to some feature of the region—a mountain, river, cave system, or glade. Imagery: maps of the region, distinctive animals of the region, protectors of the region.
19: Fire Cult	Worships the destructive power and potential of flame, perhaps secretly or open and aggressively. Imagery: candles, bonfires, oil, "eternal" flames, fire-friendly creatures.
20: Artifact Cult	Pledges to guard the location (or the secret of the location) of a particular artifact or item. Imagery: the artifact, the first guardians, the location, the defenses thereof.

Deities (d100)

Sometimes the god or goddess to whom a particular item, temple, or acolyte is dedicated is best left to chance. Roll here to determine the deity, based on their domain of influence.

1: Life

2: Sun

3: Death

4: Harvest

5: Community

6: Law & Order

7: Chaos

8: Trickery

9: Communication

10: Beauty

11: Love

12: Thunder

13: Winter

14: Summer

15: Autumn

16: Spring

17: Immortality

18: Rain

19: Plants

20: Animals

21: Water & the Sea

22: Sky

23: Hearth & Home

24: Fire

25: Forge

26: Travel

27: Magic

28: Knowledge

29: Art

30: Nature

31: Light

32: Luck

33: War

34: Protection

35: Craft & Artifice

36: Earth & Stone

37: Darkness

38: Destruction

39: Glory

40: Healing

41: Good

42: Evil

43: Freedom

44: Madness

45: Weather

46: Strength

47: The Hunt

48: Rivers & Floods

49: Birds

50: Insects & Vermin

51: The Moon

52: Cats

53: Grain

54: Fertility

55: Childbirth

56: Wisdom

57: Farming

58: Wine

59: Revelry

60: Royalty & Nobility

61: Trade & Merchants

62: Coin & Wealth

63: Secrets

64: Mysteries & Puzzles

65: Thieves

66: Misfortune

67: Time

68: Foresight

69: Emotions

70: Imagination

71: Local Nation

72: Local City

73: Stars

74: Forests

75: Mountains

76: Sleep

77: Honor & Oaths

78: Dawn

79: Night

80: Food & Eating

81: Hospitality

82: Exploration

83: Nature

84: Fields

85: The Underworld

86: The Needy

87: Lost & Forgotten Things

88: Eyes & Vision

89: Lies

90: Justice

91: Writing

92: Cattle & Livestock

93: Comedy & Jokes

94: Rebirth

95: Dogs

96: Mothers

97: Fathers

98: Disease & Sickness

99: Dead God (re-roll)

100: Unknown/Nameless God

Supernatural Beasts (d100)

Monsters, or at least the legends about such supernatural beasts, plague most fantasy worlds. Perhaps a monster has appeared in town, or perhaps the corpse or head of such a beast decorates the mantle of a home. Maybe a particular piece of treasure or art depicts a mythical creature. Roll here to generate a random fantasy monster on the fly.

1: Griffon

2: Basilisk

3: Medusa

4: Yeti

5: Sphinx

6: Chimera

7: Golem

8: Giant

9: Valkyrie

10: Dryad

11: Siren

12: Goblin

13: Hag

14: Unicorn

15: Hydra

16: Minotaur

17: Dragon

18: Kraken

19: Demon

20: Merfolk

21: Duergar

22: Ogre

23: Mummy

24: Pegasus

25: Hippocampus

26: Giant Tunnelworm

27: Roc

28: Satyr

29: Ghost

30: Lich

31: Vampire

32: Werewolf

33: Shambling Plant

34: Giant Serpent

35: Faerie/Sprite

36: Troll

37: Harpy

38: Zombie

39: Will-o-Wisp

40: Giant Wolf

41: Lizardfolk

42: Orc

43: Elemental

44: Serpentfolk

45: Shadow Creature

46: Barghest

47: Dwarf

48: Kappa

49: Centaur

50: Alien Entity

51: Naga

52: Changeling

53: Banshee

54: Brownie

55: Hippogriff

56: Cockatrice

57: Manticore

58: Nymph

59: Phoenix

60: Gargoyle

61: Sylph

62: Wraith

63: Treefolk

64: Fury

65: Lamassu

66: Ghoul

67: Gnome

68: Boggart

68: Elf

69: Ooze

70: Gorgon

71: Kitsune

72: Grindylow

73: Hellhound

74: Giant Spider

75: Cyclops

76: Homunculus

77: Rakshasa

78: Efreet

79: Jackalope

80: Bugbear

81: Kelpie

82: Gremlin

83: Undine

84: Troglodyte

85: Lamia

86: Sea Monster

87: Merrow

88: Cerberus

89: Naiad

90: Angel/Celestial

91: Revenant

92: Salamander

93: Kobold

94: Faun

95: Djinn

96: Wyvern

97: Nightmare

98: Gnoll

99: Giant Bear

100: Tarasque

Property

Picking Pockets (d100)

Every hapless bystander on the street is likely carrying something in their pockets, beltpouch, or backpack. Unfortunately for them, characters have a habit of attempting to relieve them of said possessions. Roll here to find out what a random townsperson is carrying in their pockets, adding to the roll in accordance with the wealth of the individual in question.

Wealth:

Impoverished: +0 | **Low:** +10 | **Average:** +20 | **High:** +30 | **Noble:** +40

1-10: Random Garbage

11: Lucky Charm

12: Wooden Bowl

13: Ticket/Receipt

14: Firewood Pieces

15: Drinking Horn

16: Comb/Brush

17: Toy (Dice, ball and jacks, etc.)

18: Holy Symbol/Token

19: Bar of Soap

20: Leather Straps

21: Printed Hand-Out, Badly Smudged

22: Blank Parchment

23: Worn, Moldy Waterskin

24: Food Item

25: 1d4 Pieces of Chalk

26: Small Candle

27: Small Flute or Musical Instrument

28: Buckle

29: Ball of Twine

30: Small Utility Knife

31: Single Key

32: Deck of Playing Cards

33: Shovel

34: Iron Skillet

35: Small Stew Cauldron

36: Wooden Mallet

37: Flint & Steel

38: 1d6 Sewing Needles

39: 1d6 Sheets of Blank Parchment

40: Waterskin

41: Tobacco and Pipe

42: Vial of Ink

43: Tinderbox

44: Whetstone

45: Jug of Milk

46: Soft Cap/Hat

47: Small Mirror

48: Coil of (1d6 x 10) Feet of Rope

49: Handkerchief

50: 1d4 Bottles of Lamp Oil

51: Sheaf of 5d12 Sheets of Blank Parchment

52: Note with Unimportant Writing

53: Small Lamp

54: 1d4 Quills

55: Iron Scissors

56: Small Book

57: 1d4 Torches

58: Hammer

59: Bag of 2d20 Nails

60: Wineskin

61: 1d6 Candles

62: Bottle of Ink

63: 1d4 Chisels

64: Hunting Trap

65: 1d6 Feet of Chain

66: Iron Tongs

67: Tobacco Pouch

68: Bottle of Perfume/Cologne

69: 1d8 Bottles of Oil

70: Spectacles/Monacle

71-73: Handful of Copper Coins (1d6)

74-76: Pouch of Copper Coins (1d20)

77-79: Bag of Copper Coins (10d10)

80-82: Handful of Silver Coins (1d6)

83-85: Pouch of Silver Coins (1d20)

86-88: Bag of Silver Coins (10d10)

89-92: Handful of Gold Coins (1d6)

93-96: Pouch of Gold Coins (1d20)

97-99: Bag of Gold Coins (10d10)

100: Handful of Electrum Coins (1d6)

101: Pouch of Electrum Coins (1d20)

102: Bag of Electrum Coins (10d10)

103: Handful of Platinum Coins (1d6)

104: Pouch of Platinum Coins (1d20)

105: Bag of Platinum Coins (10d10)

106-111: Melee Weapon (see page 136)

112-115: Ranged Weapon (see page 135)

116: Armor (see page 137)

117: 1 Small, Cheap Gem

118: Pouch of Small, Cheap Gems (1d4)

119: Bag of Small, Cheap Gems (4d4)

120: 1 Small, Valuable Gem

121: Pouch of Small, Valuable Gems (1d4)

122: Bag of Small, Valuable Gems (4d4)

123: 1 Large, Valuable Gem

124: Pouch of Large, Valuable Gems (1d4)

125: Bag of Large, Valuable Gems (4d4)

126: Piece of Small, Cheap Jewelry

127: Piece of Small, Valuable Jewelry

128: Piece of Large, Valuable Jewelry

129: Key Ring (3d10 keys)

130: 2d12 Trade Bars (Copper)

131: 2d12 Trade Bars (Silver)

132: 2d12 Trade Bars (Gold)

133: 2d12 Trade Bars (Platinum)

134: Map of the Region

135: Valuable Book

136: Interesting Note

137: Interesting Map

138: Semi-Skeleton Key (Opens 5% of all doors)

139: Skeleton Key (Opens all doors)

140: Thief-Catcher (Small trap to catch the fingers of pickpockets)

Garbage (d100)

Whether they are intentionally rooting around in the garbage or are simply taking refuge in the refuse, sometimes even the bravest adventurers find themselves waist-deep in trash. Roll here if it becomes necessary to find out what is the predominant or nearest item of garbage to be found.

1: Apple Core

2: Wet Paper

3: Used Greasy Rags

4: Feces-Stained Clothes

5: Wet Animal Dung

6: Dry Human Excrement

7: Dry Animal Dung

8: Torn Cloth Bag

9: Broken Axe Handle

10: Broken Axe Blade

11: Broken Sword Hilt

12: Broken Sword Blade

13: Broken Knife Hilt

14: Broken Knife Blade

15: Broken Shield Handle

16: Broken Shield Scrap

17: Broken Armor Scrap (Light)

18: Broken Armor Scrap (Medium)

19: Broken Armor Scrap (Heavy)

20: Broken Armor Scrap (Plate mail)

21: Broken Wand Piece

22: Broken Orb Fragment

23: Broken Bow Fragment

24: Broken Arrow/Bolt

25: Torn-Up Book

26: Burnt Book

27: Burnt-Up Firewood Scraps

28: Piles of Ashes

29: Burning Cinders

30: Old, Used-Up Coal

31: Broken Spear Handle

32: Broken Spear Tip

33: Spoiled Milk

34: Spoiled Wine

35: Spoiled Meat

36: Dinner Bones

37: Butcher's Scraps

38: Wet Human Excrement

39: Empty Wine Bottle

40: Empty Potion Bottle

41: Empty, Chipped Flagon

42: Empty, Bent Tankard

43: Chipped, Discarded Crockery

44: Broken Cutlery

45: Dead, Rotting Animal

46: Old, Moldy Clothes

47: Vomit-Covered Tunic

48: Melon Rinds

49: Cornhusks

50: Broken Crockery

51: Broken Wine Bottles

52: Broken Glass

53: Torn Leather Bag

54: Empty Purse

55: Copper Coin

56: Handful of Copper Coins

57: Bloodstained Clothing

58: Various Fruit Skins

59: Heaps of Congealed Fat

60: Pools of Cooking Oil

61: Sand/Dirt

62: Discarded Newsleaf (Recent)

63: Discarded Newsleaf (Old and dated)

64: Discarded Pamphlet

65: Discarded Letter

66: Left Boot with Holes

67: Right Shoe with Missing Strap

68: Bit of String

69: Strip of Leather

70: Spool of Old Twine

71: Twenty Feet of Old Rope

72: Old Military Signet/Badge

73: Hair/Fur Shavings

74: Jagged, Broken Piece of Metal

75: Lump of Discarded Pig Iron

76: Old Bucket

77: Split, Broken Bucket

78: Torn Raincloak

79: Dead Leaves/Vegetation

80: Broken-Down Crates

81: Chunk of Stone

82: Mud

83: Empty Barrel

84: Broken-Down Barrel

85: Barrel Flinders

86: Empty Crate

87: Rusted Nails

88: Old, Worn Key

89: Old Ring

90: Belt Buckle

91: Fishbones

92: Unique/Strange Alchemical Mixture

93: Toxic Alchemical Mixture

94: Human Corpse (Old bones)

95: Human Corpse (Freshly murdered)

96: Sleeping Old Woman

97: Drunk Youth

98: Drunk Adult Male

99: Unexpected Valuable

100: Unexpected Treasure

Simple Tools (d20)

Craftspeople have special tools, which they need to pursue their respective trades. Adventurers might seek to buy, steal, sell, or use such tools in town, and sometimes they aren't picky about what tool they get their hands on. Roll here to see what random tools are lying around a workshop, a worker's bag, or a supply store.

1: Carpenter's Hammer

2: Wood Axe

3: Farmer's Sickle

4: Whittling Knife

5: Handsaw

6: Trowel

7: Auger

8: Harrow

9: Chisel

10: Pitchfork

11: Shears

12: Spade

13: Tongs

14: Pickaxe

15: Plough

16: Brush

17: Threshing Flail

18: Rake

19: Sewing Needle

20: Small Utility Knife

Advanced Tools (d20)

Some tools are used in rare trades and professions. These tools tend to be more advanced, larger, and more expensive than simple tools. Roll here to see what advanced tools turn up in a specialist shop or expensive supply store.

1: Abacus

2: Acid

3: Bridle

4: Incense

5: Calligrapher's Quill

6: Compass

7: Censer

8: Climbing Pitons

9: Lump of Sealing Wax

10: Perfume

11: Dye

12: Fishing Tackle

13: Grappling Hook

14: Bottle of Ink

15: Spyglass

16: Ladder

17: Jeweler's Eye

18: Bullseye Lantern

19: Signet Ring

20: Explosives (Charcoal)

Ranged Weapons (d100)

Adventurers are always looking to scavenge or upgrade to new weapons. Roll here to see what random ranged weapons a character finds in an armory, barracks, or ready-room.

1–10: Throwing Knife

11–18: Javelin

19–25: Spear

26–32: Throwing Axe

33–35: Hand Crossbow

36–44: Light Crossbow

45–50: Arbalest (Heavy Crossbow)

51: Repeater Crossbow

52–61: Shortbow

62–68: Longbow

69–73: Dart

74–83: Sling

84–86: Blowgun

87–90: Net

91–95: Composite Bow

96–97: Boomerang

98–99: Bola

100: Early Firearm

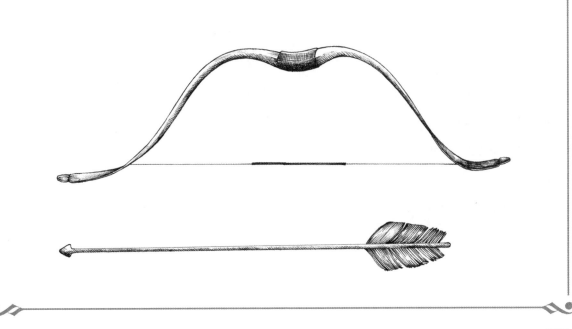

Melee Weapons (d100)

Adventurers are always looking to scavenge or upgrade to new weapons. Roll here to see what random melee weapons a character finds in an armory, barracks, or ready-room.

1-5: Longsword

6-10: Shortsword

11-14: Greatsword

15-19: Dagger

20-24: Knife

25: Punching Dagger

26: Spiked Gauntlet

27: Whip

28: Bastard Sword

29-30: Rapier

31-32: Scimitar

33-36: Spear

37-38: Longspear

39-41: Polearm (Halberd, etc.)

42-45: Mace

46-49: Battleaxe

50-53: Handaxe

54-56: Greataxe

57-60: Club

61-65: Quarterstaff

66-68: Flail

69-72: Morningstar

73-75: Maul

76-78: Warhammer

79: Trident

80-82: Sickle

83-84: Scythe

85-86: Greatclub

87-88: Pitchfork

89-90: Light Hammer

91-92: Lance

93: Brass Knuckles

94: Shortspear

95-96: Sap

97-98: Cutlass

99: Sword Cane

100: Caltrops

Armor (d100)

Adventurers are always looking to scavenge or upgrade to new armor. Roll here to see what random armor a character finds in an armory, barracks, or ready-room.

1-7: Padded Armor

8-11: Cloth Armor

12-17: Leather Armor

18-23: Studded Leather

24-29: Hide Armor

30-34: Breastplate

35-38: Halfplate

39-44: Chain Shirt

45-50: Scale Mail

51-55: Ring Mail

56-61: Chain Mail

62-65: Splint Mail

66-68: Banded Mail

69-70: Plate Mail

71: Ceremonial Armor

72: Natural Armor (Leaves, silk, chitin)

73-74: Wooden Armor

75-80: Buckler

81-85: Small Metal Shield

86-88: Heavy Metal Shield

89-94: Small Wooden Shield

95-98: Heavy Wooden Shield

99-100: Tower Shield

Clothing (d20)

Sometimes rifling through a wardrobe or satchel might accidentally turn up articles of clothing. Other times, characters might be deliberately looking to strip down people or locations for clothing. Fun and profit can ensue when you walk a mile in another man's shoes; roll here to see what random items of clothing characters might come across while searching.

1: Underclothes/Smallclothes

2: Scandalous Lingerie

3: Cloaks

4: Mantles

5: Furs

6: Gloves

7: Boots

8: Shoes

9: Caps/Hoods

10: Tunics

11: Trousers/Drawers

12: Leggings/Stockings

13: Belts/Girdles

14: Dresses

15: Nightwear

16: Religious Clothing (Coverings, shawls)

17: Formal Dress

18: Military Uniforms

19: Fine Clothes w/ Sentimental Value (e.g., Wedding dress)

20: Old Clothes w/ Sentimental Value (e.g., Grandma's cowl)

Musical Instruments (d20)

Not every bard can afford to rely on their singing voice alone, and rare and exotic instruments might set one musician apart from another, both as an act and as a memorable encounter. Roll here to see what the band is playing or what instrument an adventurer lifts off of a musical mark.

1: Lute

2: Fife

3: Harp

4: Fiddle

5: Mandolin

6: Trumpet

7: Flute

8: Shawm

9: Drum

10: Bells

11: Timbrel

12: Tabor

13: Horn

14: Cymbals

15: Lyre

16: Rebec

17: Bagpipes

18: Dulcimer

19: Harpsichord

20: Organ (Portable or stationary)

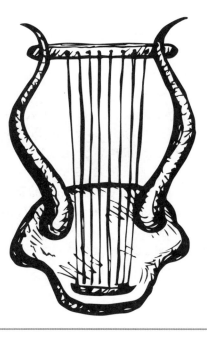

Books (d20)

Whether pillaging an ancient library or simply lifting a title off of the nearest book stand, adventurers might stumble across unexpected books and tomes. Roll here to see what kind of book they find.

Book	Description
1: Encyclopedia	This book gives insight into a number of different topics but only offers a light (and largely incomplete) overview of the vast breadth of material it attempts to cover.
2: Bestiary	A list of monstrous creatures—perhaps merely exotic or poorly studied animals, or beings far more supernatural.
3: History	An account of the history of a nation, town, or people. It claims to be told from an objective perspective, but this claim is unlikely to hold up.
4: Traveler's Guide	This books gives advice regarding a specific country, town, or region to best prepare travelers for journeys through the area.
5: Geography	Information regarding a region, land, or continent, including possible environmental dangers and flora or fauna that might be encountered.
6: Biography	An account of the life of a famous hero, political figure, military general, or other well-known individual.
7: Illuminated Book	This book is filled with pictures. They may be exquisitely crafted or crude, but they dominate the book more than the words. Roll again to see what genre this illustrated text falls into.
8: Prayer Book	A collection of prayers for a particular religion or god, or prayers dedicated to many different gods intended for a particular individual.
9: Children's Book	A collection of stories and/or songs intended for young children. It may include instructional help for beginner readers.
10: Poetry	A full sampling of the work of a well-respected poet-bard of the land. The poetry is highly praised among the town's cultured elite.
11: Cookbook	A list of recipes for different meals, including some exotic or lost recipes that may require equally exotic or lost ingredients.
12: Handbook	Advice on how to best pursue a particular trade, craft, or art. The thoughts here were recorded by master artisans, not all of whom were experts at clearly conveying their thoughts.
13: Fiction	An enjoyable and divertive look into a silly social situation, tense melodrama, or exciting adventure tale.

Book	Description
14: Epic	A famed classic or an epic poem dedicated to a famous war or other chapter of mythic history in the world's past.
15: Religious Text	An account of the religious beliefs of a particular faith or sect in town. It may be an accurate transcription of their beliefs or a heretical account.
16: Racy Fantasy	This book is from someone's "private collection" and may give interesting and much-regretted insight into an individual's private imaginings.
17: Tome of Some Magical Power	A grimoire of magical knowledge, highly useful to a spellcaster, but not so much to anyone else.
18: Tome of Dark Magical Power	Contains dark and twisted secrets best not known by mortal minds. It will corrupt anyone who tries to use it and quietly tempt those who do not.
19: Tome of Great Magical Power	Possesses a great deal of magical power, even in the hands of one unaccomplished in magic. It's just that much more dangerous!
20: Enchanted Talking Book	This book speaks for itself. Literally. And it won't. Shut. Up. Roll again to see what topics this book keeps talking about.

Sentimental Items (d20)

Some items are carried by their owners not because of their great value or great power, but for sentimental reasons. Roll here to see what kind of a sentimental item a townsperson might be carrying, storing in a safe space, or simply have an emotional attachment to.

1: Locket

2: Jewel

3: Necklace

4: Ring

5: Preserved Hair

6: Dried Flower

7: Scrawled Paper (With quote or poem)

8: Handmade Cup

9: Hand-Carved Figurine

10: Lucky Animal's Foot

11: Perfumed Love Note

12: Seashell Collection

13: Small Statuette

14: Bone Talisman

15: Chipped Runestone

16: Old Armor Fragment

17: Small Framed Painting

18: Etched Holy Symbol

19: Page from a Favorite Book

20: Journal/Diary

Magic Items (d20)

Magic, or at least the appearance of magic, is a temptation few can pass up. Plenty of con artists and tricksters might claim to barter in enchanted property, and some might even be telling the truth. Roll here to see what kind of unique magical items might be found for sale or have become the source of local legends.

1: Magic Ring

2: Magic Harp

3: Magic Jewel

4: Magic Rod

5: Magic Eye

6: Magic Belt/Girdle

7: Magic Necklace

8: Magic Boots

9: Magic Wand

10: Magic Cloak

11: Magic Cauldron

12: Magic Glove

13: Magic Bell

14: Magic Shield

15: Magic Sword

16: Magic Helm

17: Magic Armor

18: Magic Staff

19: Magic Bow

20: Magic Amulet

Jail Cell Items (d20)

Prisons are not typically known for containing loose lockpicks or convenient weapons lying around. That being said, characters might try to scrape together a solution out of whatever desperate scraps they can find. Roll here to determine what those desperate scraps might be.

1: Tooth/Fang

2: Animal Bone

3: Human Bone

4: Wooden Dish

5: Metal Bowl

6: Braid of Hair

7: Small Live Animal

8: Shiv

9: Length of Chain

10: Coin

11: Coil of Rope

12: Heavy Stone

13: Small Stone

14: Rusty Nail

15: Shackle

17: Rat Droppings

18: Dead Rat

19: Letter Left by a Previous Inmate

20: Hidden Magical Item

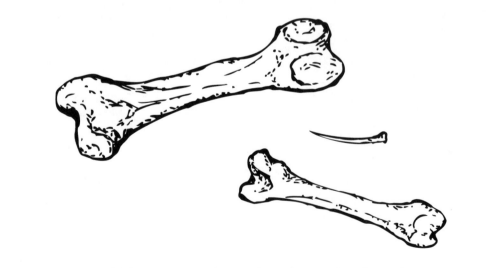

Wagon Contents (d20)

Sometimes the characters will not always look before they leap. When free-falling to street level from some window or rooftop, it can be helpful to aim for a nearby cart—hopefully with something soft. Roll here to determine what manner of wagon contents break their fall—or break them instead.

1: Hay (Soft)

2: Raw Uncut Stone (Hard)

3: Straw (Soft)

4: Masonry Bricks (Hard)

5: Cloth/Fabric (Soft)

6: Raw Lumber (Hard)

7: Corpses (Sort of soft)

8: Glassware (Hard, sharp)

9: Hide/Skins (Soft)

10: Pottery (Hard, breakable)

11: Fruits/Vegetables (Soft, breakable)

12: Raw Ore (Hard)

13: Animals/Livestock (Soft, breakable)

14: Fashioned Iron (Hard, sharp)

15: Meat/Grains (Soft)

16: Weapons (Hard, very sharp)

17: Passengers (Soft, breakable)

18: Fashioned Wood (Hard, breakable)

19: Pillows (Soft)

20: Precious Metals (Hard)

Barrel Contents (d20)

Barrels are a staple of the medieval era for so many reasons. Beyond simple storage, the potential for barrels to be used as projectile ammunition, hiding spaces, obstacles, and cover is limited only by the imagination of the characters who get their hands on them. If it suddenly becomes relevant what a particular barrel is filled with, roll here.

1: Garbage

2: Empty

3: Empty but Putrid

4: Fertilizer

5: Water

6: Wine

7: Wooden Staves

8: Weapons

9: Straw

10: Oil

11: Tallow

12: Ale

13: Cider

14: Fruit

15: Ammunition (Quarrels, Arrows)

16: Ammunition (Gunpowder, Cannonballs, Bullets)

17: Whiskey

18: Sack (Sherry)

19: Nails

20: Hot Soup

Vault/Safe Contents (d20)

Every thief in town dreams of robbing the mansions and estates of the nobility. But with wealth comes access to advanced security, and not every thief can crack a vault or a safe. Of course, some can. Characters often target the rich and corrupt, and might break into a vault that you didn't expect them to break into. When that happens, roll on this table to generate the contents of a vault or safe inside of a well-off citizen's home.

1: Deeds to the House the Safe Is In

2: Deeds to Real Estate Elsewhere in Town

3: Deeds to Real Estate Outside of Town (A cabin, mill, tower, etc.)

4: Gold Ingots

5: Silver Ingots

6: Ingots of a Rare and Unusual Metal

7: Iron Ingots

8: Precious Gems

9: Precious Jewelry

10: Valuable Paintings

11: Valuable Tapestries

12: Family Bones/Urn

13: Valuable Weapon (Usable, see page 136)

14: Valuable Weapon (Ceremonial, see page 136)

15: Valuable Armor/Shield (Usable, see page 137)

16: Valuable Armor/Shield (Ceremonial, see page 137)

17: Holy Lost Relic of a Good Religion

18: Dark Phylactery of an Ancient Evil

19: A Trophy from a Rare Beast

20: Proof of Secret Nobility/Inheritance

Graves (d20)

Graverobbing has a long-standing history, even in worlds where dead loved ones are not regularly being raised back to life (or unlife). It can also be one of the easiest ways to steal, the dead being notoriously bad with property. Roll here to generate the graves (and contents thereof) for random local townsfolk.

Grave	Description
1: Agatha Goldenleaf	Aged 68. Herbalist. Grave has various healing herbs growing from the soil. Contains 1d4 bushels of exotic herbs with rare restorative properties.
2: Martha Salbar	Aged 44. Guard and Bounty Hunter. Grave describes her heroic exploits in town solving crimes and taking on villains. Contains high-quality, well-preserved longbows, elven-made leather armor, and a troll's skull.
3: Lars Breyburn	Aged 56. Farmer. Fought in a nearby battle over 200 years ago for a lord whose cause was lost to history. Buried near his two sons. Contains a rusted longsword and suit of chainmail.
4: Lord Hadderhew	Aged 77. Local Noble. Elaborate gravestone notes that he built the local keep (inside or near town). Contains an elegant silver crown and valuable ring with the of symbol the local nobility (albeit out of date), as well as a map depicting a secret tunnel into the keep's dungeons.
5: Vlad Hornbreaker	Aged 36. Soldier. According to his mausoleum wall, he died in a famous battle and was buried in his hometown with the highest honors. Contains an enchanted longsword and a set of beautiful plate mail armor.
6: Diego Crucibus	Aged 331. A magician and alchemist, famed for almost perfecting the secret of eternal life. Contains a bronze locket with a minuscule secret compartment, inside of which is contained a scrap of the alchemist's secret longevity formula.
7: Aileen Moskwood	Aged 51. Baker. Contains a wooden pipe, a tin flute, and a silver necklace with a glass sphere, inside of which is embedded a strange fang.
8: Sarah "Sapphire" Underton	Aged 38. Occupation Unknown. Contains a hand crossbow, leather armor, and fake magical boots of sneaking. In a secret compartment at the foot of the coffin are real magical boots of sneaking and a large bag of gold.
9: Isabella Nightsong	Aged 243. Elven Woodcarver. Contains a necklace, a menagerie of animals, and a model ship, all exquisitely carved of beautiful rare wood.

Grave	Description
10: Captain Sarto Sandor	Aged 55. Merchant Captain. Contains a chest with a small cache of gold and a map leading to a buried treasure—not necessarily on an island.
11: Aldo Henwick	Aged 45. Tailor. Contains a jade pendant and a copper ring, as well as a silver tooth in the skeleton's mouth. The beautiful clothing he was buried in has mostly rotted away.
12: Nyla Abernis	Aged 14. Daughter to Hammond Abernis, local farmer. Died of a local plague. Contains a wooden painted doll and a small engraved prayer book.
13: Christoph Pyler	Aged 7. Son to Amie and Talia Pyler. Killed during a raid on a nearby village. Contains a pair of gold coins that were set onto the child's eyes.
14: Nadia Everdell	Aged 1 month. Daughter to Angus and Aliana Everdell. Died of starvation during a famine long ago. Contains a tattered baby blanket.
15: Corbin Newell	Aged 33. Adventurer. Died fighting a local monster who still threatens the town (the monster's image adorns the grave). Contains a pair of healing potions and a jeweled ring, left by Corbin's old teammates.
16: Princess Augustana Matoria	Aged 25. Her elaborate mausoleum is adorned with recreations of her beauty in sculptures and paintings. Contains 1d8 pieces of valuable artwork.
17: Joseph Reiner	Aged 45. Writer. Contains a silver necklace and the tattered remnants of Joseph's unfinished manuscript. As Joseph has become posthumously famous, his manuscript may be valuable to the right buyer.
18: Lindell Hawthorne	Aged 57. Healer. Religious iconography. Contains a variety of curative ointments, as well as a magic wood and bone charm that is actually quite effective at warding off a certain kind of evil spirit.
19: Fredrick Belloise	Aged 43. Builder. Contains an expert crafting hammer and a small copper ring, as well as a map of the town with notes on which buildings have the least stable structures.
20: Anna Halifax	Aged 44. Juggler/Performer. Contains dozens of precious necklaces and bracelets, as well as an emerald-studded ring and a miniature (possibly magical) silver harp.

Alchemical Components (d100)

Alchemy and other sciences of the time required plenty of specialized components and ingredients. Some of these chemicals are ordinary and harmless, others have unique, interesting, useful, or even dangerous qualities. Of course, mixing and matching can be fun too! Roll here to stock an alchemy lab or shop with interesting components and supplies.

1: Fresh Water

2: Salt

3: Sulfur

4: Alcohol

5: Saltpeter

6: Oil

7: Honey

8: Cream

9: Milk

10: Vinegar

11: Salt Water

12: Wine

13: Beer

14: Aqua Regia

15: Chlorine

16: Mercury

17: Gold

18: Oil of Vitriol

19: Copper

20: Chalk

21: Fool's Gold

22: Pine Tree Sap

23: Crushed Flowers

24: Acacia Gum

25: Mercury

26: Lead

27: Quicklime

28: Lye

29: Verdigris

30: White Arsenic

31: Gypsum Stone

32: Butter of Antimony

33: Antimony (Oxychloride)

34: Realgar

35: Corrosive Sublimate

36: Aqua Fortis (Nitric Acid)

37: Hydrochloric Acid

38: Silver

39: Iron

40: Steel

41: Local Herbs

42: Foreign Herbs

43: Exotic Herbs

44: Asparagus

45: Pine

46: Local Mushrooms

47: Foreign Mushrooms

48: Exotic Mushrooms

49: Sesame

50: Kola Nuts

51: Cinnabar

52: Myrrh

53: Phosphorus

54: Urea

55: Magnesium

56: Greek Fire

57: Animal Claw

58: Beehive Combs

59: Bone Meal

60: Powdered Insects

61: Tiny Eggs

62: Moss

63: Lichen

64: Garlic

65: Animal Beaks

66: Feathers

67: Human Flesh

68: Berries

69: Pearl

70: Powdered Tusk

71: Spider Eggs

72: Spider Webbing

73: Animal Fat

74: Cotton

75: Wheat

76: Wormwood

77: Wolfsbane

78: Nightshade

79: Aqua Vitae (Ethanol)

80: Bismuth

81: Bitumen (Asphalt)

82: Cadmia

83: Glass of Antimony

84: Green Vitriol

85: Sugar of Lead

86: Powdered Animal Bone

87: Powdered Human Bone

88: Amber

89: Tin

90: Cobalt

91: Coal

92: Sugar

93: Platinum

94: Zinc

95: Animal Venom

96: Powerful Antidote

97: Deadly Poison

98: Essential Oils (???)

99: Philosopher's Stone (Fake)

100: Philosopher's Stone (Real...?)

Magical Alchemy Components (d100)

In fantasy worlds, alchemy goes above and beyond the ordinary mixing of chemicals. Supernatural and magical ingredients are an important part of the mystic work that the alchemists participate in; such ingredients are especially rare, valuable, and powerful. Roll here to see what magical ingredients your alchemist has stocked.

1: Vampire Fangs

2: Unicorn Horn

3: Phoenix Feather

4: Ghoul Talons

5: Mermaid Hair

6: Cerberus Fangs

7: Harpy Talon

8: Strand of Medusa Hair

9: Hemlock

10: Basilisk Scale

11: Gorgon Eye

12: Demon Heart

13: Nightshade Petals

14: Wolfsbane

15: Petal of the Everbloom

16: Dwarven Grease

17: Ectoplasm

18: Powdered Elf Ears

19: Everburning Cinders

20: Giant's Tooth

21: Nymph Sap

22: Giant Spider Eggs

23: Lich Dust

24: Angel Hair

25: Angel Feather

26: Beetle Eyes

27: Devil Tongue

28: Dwarf Liver

29: Goblin Tooth

30: Bugbear Hair

31: Dragon Tooth

32: Dragon Blood

33: Demon Ichor

34: Angel Blood

35: Elemental Core

36: Newt Eyes

37: Frog Toes

38: Bat Wool

37: Dog Tongues

38: Snake Tongues

39: Blind-Worm Stingers

40: Lizard Legs

41: Owl Wings

42: Human Soul

43: Human Brain

44: Human Bonemeal

45: Human Brains

46: Efreeti Embers

47: Hand of a Thief

48: Tongue of an Honest Man

49: Harpy Feathers

50: Magically Resonant Ore

51: Werewolf Teeth

52: Jackalope Hairs

54: Dryad Bark

55: Faerie Wings

56: Pixie Dust

57: Dark Elf Blood

58: Gargoyle Shards

59: Caterpillars/Worms

60: Witch Heart

61: Bezoar

62: Necromancer's Skull

63: Minotaur Horn

64: Sphinx Eye

65: Centaur Hoof

66: Rakshasa Claw

67: Zombie Rot

68: Djinn Dust

69: Wormwood

70: Chimera Claw

71: Hydra Blood

72: Hydra Fang

73: Giant Spider Silk

74: Mandrake Root

75: Griffon Feathers

76: Hippogriff Feathers

77: Ground Hippogriff Hooves

78: Satyr Horns

79: Hag Skin

80: Hellhound Fang

81: Kraken Ink

82: Crocodile Heart

83: Kobold Toe

84: Lamia Lips

85: Troll Flesh

86: Venomous Toadstools

87: Pearl Dust

88: Wyvern Sting

89: Manticore Spines

90: Mummy Dust

91: Frog Brains

92: Ginger

93: Eel Eyes

94: Naga Scales

95: Ogre Toe

96: Pegasus Feathers

97: Roc Feathers

98: Giant Snake Venom

99: Sphinx Feathers

100: Sacred Moly

Herbs (d20)

Herbs and plants don't only grow in the wilderness—especially in small villages, it's common for people to maintain gardens with useful flora. Roll here to see what is growing in someone's yard or what is in stock at the local herbalist.

1: Sage

2: Rosemary

3: Thyme

4: Lavender

5: Dill

6: Basil

7: Hyssop

8: Pennyroyal

9: Parsley

10: Mugwort

11: Chamomile

12: Oregano

13: Rue

14: Comfrey

15: St John's-wort

16: Caraway

17: Marjoram

18: Lemon Balm

19: Peppermint

20: Wormwood

Poisons (d20)

Whether shopping in the black market or looting a would-be assassin, certain adventurers are always on the lookout for a poison that will give them the extra edge. Roll here to generate your own unique poison with its own effects. Decide how many times to roll for a given poison, how potent the effect, and of course, how much the label (if any) says!

1: Sleeping

2: Knocking Out

3: Forgetfulness

4: Paralysis

5: Blindness

6: Deafness

7: Numbing

8: Clumsiness

9: Weakness

10: Catatonia

11: Nausea

12: Truth Serum

13: Obedience

14: Loss of Focus

15: Itching/Rashes

16: Ego Loss

17: Blurry Vision

18: Slow Death

19: Painful Death

20: Sudden Death

Menu Items (d100)

Whether they stay at the lowliest cottage or the finest inn, characters on the road need to eat. Well-traveled adventurers, newly returned to civilization, might be eager to eat some home cooking—but not all menus are created equal, and one can often taste the difference between spending a copper and a silver coin on a meal. Roll here to spice up the selection of any culinary establishment in your game. Add to the roll according to the quality of the establishment:

Quality:
Impoverished: +0 | **Low:** +10 | **Average:** +20 | **High:** +30 | **Exotic:** +40 | **Noble Banquet:** +50

1: Rat Stew

2: Bowl of Acorns

3: Acorn Bread

4: Peasant Porridge

5: Mixed Ground Nuts

6: Buckwheat Porridge

7: Bowl of Chestnuts

8: Thin Chicken Broth

9: Bread and Gruel

10: Dark Rye Bread

11: Steamed Vegetables

12: Boiled Carrots

13: Oat Porridge

14: Potato Soup

15: Cabbage Soup

16: Boiled Turnip

17: Hedgehog Stew

18: Buckwheat Biscuits

19: Bowl of Oats

20: Porcupine Soup

21: Raccoon Stew

22: Rabbit Stew

23: Roast Potatoes

24: Baked Potatoes

25: Mixed Fresh Fruit

26: Bean Broth

27: Roast Mutton

28: Vegetable Soup

29: Apple Soup

30: Hard-Boiled Eggs

31: Tomato Soup

32: Millet Biscuits

33: Roasted Cony

34: Cheese Wheel

35: Barley Cake

36: Roast Chicken

37: Pottage

38: Hazelnut Bread

39: Cooked Beetroot

40: Mixed Berries

41: Baked Beans

42: Beaver Soup

43: Roast Goat Haunch

44: Stone-Baked Cod

45: Fried Cod

46: Steamed Crab Legs

47: Cashew Bread

48: Smoked Eel

49: Smoked Cod

50: Smoked Herring

51: Honeycomb

52: Beef Stew

53: Turtle Soup

54: Trout Fillet

55: White Bread

56: Potato Bread

57: Turkey Leg

58: Turkey Breast

59: Venison Stew

60: Cooked Rice

61: Cheese Tart

62: Oatcakes

63: Simple Pasta

64: Salted Cod

65: Salted Herring

66: Roast Goose

67: Mutton Stew

68: Apple Tart

69: Dried Figs

70: Dried Dates

71: Almond Cakes

72: Bread Trenchers (For stew)

73: Whey Cheese

74: Grilled Chicken Breast

75: Dried Legumes

76: Mincemeat Pie

77: Sugar Biscuit

78: Garlic Soup

79: Onion Soup

80: Plum Pudding

81: Cooked Peas

82: Pork Sausage

83: Clam Chowder

84: Roast Horse Haunch

85: Roast Quail

86: Roast Partridge

87: Roast Duck

88: Duck Stew

89: Steamed Oysters

90: Steamed Mussels

91: Stewed Lentils

92: Cheese Omelet

93: Vegetable Omelet

94: Dried Leeks

95: Honeycake

96: Beefsteak

97: Egg Pie (Quiche)

98: Salmon Steak

99: Dried Carp

99: Bacon Rashers

100: Smoked Pike

101: Venison Stew

102: Roast Heron

103: Swan Breast

104: Venison Roast

105: Stewed Mushrooms

106: Sugared Almonds

107: Almond Pudding

108: Rice Tart

109: Roast Pheasant

110: Fig Pie

111: Boiled Sausage

112: Strawberry Pasty

113: Curd Cheese

114: Stewed Pork

115: Eel Fillet

116: Dried Artichokes

117: Roast Pork

118: Braised Duck

119: Blueberry Pasty

120: Onion Omelet

121: Smoked Lamb

122: Sweetcake

123: Smoked Carp

124: Smoked Bear

125: Steamed Scallops

126: Salted Boar

127: Fried Herring

128: Roasted Mushrooms

129: Dried Plums

130: Braised Pheasant

131: Roast Bear

132: Beef Sausage

133: Roasted Grouse

134: Sugar Cubes

135: Full Boar Roast

136: Raspberry Pasty

137: Smoked Goose

138: Orange Tart

139: Boiled Shellfish

140: Smoked Veal

141: Roast Veal

142: Smoked Venison

143: Roast Elk

144: Whale Steak

145: Cake

146: Unique Local Specialty

147: Local Exotic Food Item

148: Supernatural Vegetable (Magic Fungi, Fruit, etc.)

149: Supernatural Meat (Dragon, Unicorn, etc.)

150: Magical/Supernatural Food Item

Beverages (d20)

Nothing lets an adventurer know that they can kick up their heels and take a load off quite like a stiff drink. But not all taverns carry the same selection; a great drink menu might be what turns a taproom into the party's new favorite place to crash! Roll here to generate a full drink menu, or find out the house specialty of any culinary establishment in your game, adding to the roll according to the quality of the establishment:

Quality:

Impoverished: +0 | Low: +10 | Average: +20 | High: +30 | Exotic/Noble Banquet: +40

1: Cup of Moonshine

2: Jug of Moonshine

3: Cup of Clean Water

4: Pitcher of Clean Water

5: Pint of Grog

6: Pitcher of Grog

7: Cup of Cold Milk

8: Pint of Beer

9: Pitcher of Beer

10: Pint of Bitter

11: Pitcher of Bitter

12: Pint of Ale

13: Pitcher of Ale

14: Cup of Herbal Tea

15: Pot of Herbal Tea

16: Cup of Barley Tea

17: Pot of Barley Tea

18: Jug of Milk

19: Glass of White Wine

20: Pitcher of White Wine

21: Glass of Red Wine

22: Pitcher of Red Wine

23: Bottle of Red Wine

24: Bottle of White Wine

25: Jug of Red Wine

26: Pint of Mead

27: Pitcher of Mead

28: Pint of Stout

29: Pitcher of Stout

30: Glass of Rum

31: Glass of Whiskey

32: Glass of Brandy

33: Cup of Almond Milk

34: Cup of Warm Milk

35: Glass of Verjuice

36: Cup of Hot Mulled Wine

37: Cup of Apple Cider

38: Cup of Hot Cider

39: Pitcher of Apple Cider

40: Pitcher of Hot Cider

41: Pitcher of Hot Mulled Wine

42: Cup of Mulberry Wine

43: Pitcher of Mulberry Wine

44: Cup of Pomegranate Wine

45: Pitcher of Pomegranate Wine

46: Cup of Sack (Sherry)

47: Cup of Eggnog

48: Cup of Fresh Fruit Juice

49: Cup of Perry (Pear Cider)

50: Pitcher of Perry (Pear Cider)

51: Cup of Sweet Tea

52: Pot of Sweet Tea

53: Cup of Sage Water

54: Pitcher of Sage Water

55: Cup of Lemon Drink

56: Pitcher of Lemon Drink

57: Cup of Spiced Pomegranate Drink

58: Pitcher of Spiced Pomegranate Drink

59: Glass of Rose Soda

60: Magical Elixir-Beverage

Street Food (d20)

Not all food is sold at taverns and shops. A large enough town might have street food sold from stands, mobile carts, or individual peddlers and hawkers, especially during a large festival or street fair. Roll here to see what street food is being sold.

1: Sugar Sticks

2: Meat on a Stick

3: Rat Meat

4: Bruised Apple

5: Pork Pie

6: Baked Bread

7: Carrot Stew

8: Oysters/Cockles

9: Berries

10: Cabbage

11: Potato Hash

12: Raccoon Jerky

13: Hot Beans

14: Hot Cake/Crepe

15: Peanuts

16: Wild Nuts

17: Molasses Toffees

18: Sweetgrass

19: Chicken Haunch

20: Pickles

Thanks to my community at PWF that is so proud and wants to shout me out at all times! Thanks to Kiyan Fox for his support with the graphics and his vision for design and development.

Rich: Thank you to my father Guy and to my mother Marguerite, for teaching me about the importance of having a strong work ethic, even when no one is watching, to consistently value my talents, and to always care for and have respect for others. I watched both of you successfully navigate corporate America, no doubt dealing with toxic bosses but never wavering in your dedication to your family above all else. I continue to be inspired by you both. Thank you to my sister Galia, my brother-in-law Rodney, and my wonderful nieces Alex and Saniyah. We have been so honored to have you all in our lives and to witness your incredible successes.

I am also grateful to all my friends, extended family, and former colleagues, whose stories of dealing with toxic work cultures planted the seeds for this book. Hopefully it can be a significant contribution to creating healthy workplaces where everyone can thrive.

ABOUT THE AUTHORS

Dr. Lisa Orbé-Austin is a licensed psychologist, executive coach, and organizational consultant. Her views about career management and advancement are regularly sought by the media, and she has appeared in various outlets, such as the *New York Times*, *Forbes*, *NBC News*, *Refinery29*, and *Insight Into Diversity*. She has also been honored by LinkedIn as Top Voice in the area of Job Search & Careers and Mental Health. Dr. Orbé-Austin received her bachelor's degree in English from Boston College, her master's degree in counseling psychology from Boston College, and her PhD in counseling psychology from Columbia University.

Dr. Richard Orbé-Austin is a licensed psychologist, executive coach, and organizational consultant. He is also a former chief diversity officer and the founding director of NYU's Graduate Student Career Development Center. Dr. Orbé-Austin's opinions and writings have appeared in *Forbes*, *Fast Company*, *Diversity Executive*, and *ThriveGlobal*, among others. He received his bachelor's degree in psychology from NYU and his PhD in counseling psychology from Fordham University's Graduate School of Education.

Drs. Lisa and Richard Orbé-Austin gave a TEDx talk entitled "The Impostor Syndrome Paradox: Unleashing the Power of You." They are also the authors of *Own Your Greatness: Overcome Impostor Syndrome, Beat Self-Doubt, and Succeed in Life* (Ulysses Press, 2020).

ACKNOWLEDGMENTS

We would really like to thank and dedicate this book to all of our clients, students, and readers of our first book, *Own Your Greatness*. Thank you for trusting us with your vulnerability and desire to overcome your impostor syndrome and to show us that there was more work to do, which resulted in this book.

Thank you to Ulysses Press and Bridget Thoreson, who this time took the call from us, as we proposed this book to her, who championed the concepts and enthusiastically buoyed us to keep it moving forward. Thanks to Renee Rutledge for her thorough and thoughtful lead of the editorial process. And thanks to Kirsten Janene-Nelson for your work in the trenches with us and helping to really polish the manuscript.

Thank you always to our daughters, Nia and Maya! Your laughter, support, and encouragement to keep going when things were rough have really been integral to us finishing this book. We love you and hope you never experience impostor syndrome! You are both amazing and we are grateful to get to be part of your journey with you.

Thanks to Anna and Cristina! We are so grateful to you that it is beyond words. You make what seems like the impossible possible and always encourage us to dream bigger. We love your spirits, your passion, and your commitment. We love you!

Lisa: Thank you to my father, Francisco, who was the first organizational psychologist that I ever knew (he was actually a computer programmer, but even without the training he was amazing and inspired). His regular conversations with me about the issues he faced at work were the first moment that I understood leadership, workplace dynamics, racism in the workplace, and how to use your power to change things.

Thank you to my mother, Anna, who was the first psychologist I ever met (she was actually a stay-at-home mom). Your keen insights into family dynamics, intrapersonal functioning, and one's ability to understand the things that were happening around you to lessen their power and make you feel a sense of agency changed my life. You are a brilliant woman and I am so grateful you are my mother and teacher; you are just my love!

Thanks to my Aunt Mayda for always cheering me on! I am grateful for your constant support and your pride in me makes me overflow with gratitude.

Acknowledgments

Timm would like to thank his family, who have supported him throughout his journey. His parents, Maura and Ed, for supporting his D&D hobby even when it was concerning to do so; his siblings Brendan, Deirdre, and Bridget for being his original D&D party; and his girlfriend Linzi for helping to generate some of the best ideas for this book (and if your players come to hate the song "Me Olde Faire Lady," don't blame him).

About the Author

Timm Woods is a professional Game Master, educator, and a lifelong fan of role-playing games. He studies RPGs as outlets for creative fun, and as tools with immense learning potential. He earned his PhD at St. John's University, writing his dissertation on the connections between games and the classroom. He is passionate about working with schools and game-based education in a variety of forms.

Timm runs approximately 6 to 10 sessions of Dungeons & Dragons on a weekly basis, as well as many other RPGs. Dozens of groups of students, families, coworkers, and friends of all ages have had fun discovering the magic and fun of gaming! Learn more about Timm's work at timmwoods.com.

Stuffed Heads (d20)

Lots of taverns—not to mention quite a few shops, homes, castles, lodges, and other locations—might feature a stuffed head over the bar or mantle. Roll here to generate an interesting and unique trophy at each new location.

1: Elk

2: Boar

3: Deer

4: Eagle

5: Stag

6: Black Bear

7: Brown Bear

8: Giant Stag

9: Fish/Crustacean

10: Moose

11: Fox

12: Ape

13: Bobcat

14: Wolf

15: Lion

16: Ram

17: Elephant/Mammoth

18: Rhinoceros

19: Manufactured Taxidermy (e.g., Jackalope)

20: Supernatural Beast

Supernatural Foods (d20)

Certain establishments, wealthy homes, and noble institutions might have the means to provide foodstuffs of supernatural origins. Roll here to see what kind of interesting and strange delicacies might be on the menu.

1: Dragon's Egg Hollandaise

2: (Neutralized) Ooze Pudding

3: Phoenix Cordonbleu

4: Smoked Kraken

5: Minotaur Steak

6: Manticore Chops

7: Fried Basilisk

8: Sea Serpent Fillet

9: Unicorn Roast

10: Griffon Goulash

11: Ogre Stroganoff

12: Hippogriff Stew

13: Cockatrice Nuggets

14: Spicy Salamander Soup

15: Roc Egg Frittata

16: Cornmeal-Crusted Hydra

17: Hellhound Haunches

18: Giant-Sized Food (Roll on page 158)

19: Flying Buffalo Wings

20: Ambrosia